Making Wood Handles Hinges & Knobs

The Perfect Touch for Cabinetmaking

Alan & Gill Bridgewater

Sterling Publishing Co., Inc.
New York

Although in times past Gillian and I have both given thanks to our sons, our parents, and various friends and family who have helped us along the way, I think now it's about time I thanked Gill, my wife, for working with me on this book and the other thirty or so that have gone before. A wonderful—ouch—beautiful wife!

Alan Bridgewater

We would also like to thank all the people and companies who have helped us with tools and materials:

Jim Brewer—Research and Marketing Manager, Freud, Highpoint, North Carolina (Forstner drill bits)

Paragon Communications—Evo-Stick, Stafford, England (PVA adhesive)

Frank Cootz—Public Relations, Ryobi America Corp., Anderson, South Carolina (thickness planer)

Tim Effrem—President, Wood Carvers Supply, Englewood, Florida (woodcarving tools)

Dawn Fretz—Marketing Assistant, De-Sta-Co, Troy, Michigan (clamps)

John P. Jodkin—Vice President, Delta International Machinery Corp., Pittsburgh, Pennsylvania (band saw)

William Nelsen—President, Foredom Electric, Bethel, Connecticut (power tools)

Glen Tizzard—Draper Tools UK, Eastleigh, Hampshire, England (power tools)

Library of Congress Cataloging-in-Publication Data

Bridgewater, Alan.
    Making wood handles, hinges & knobs : the perfect touch for cabi netmaking / by Alan & Gill Bridgewater.
      p.   cm.
    Includes index.
    ISBN 0-8069-1335-5
    1. Cabinetwork. 2. Cabinet hardware. I. Bridgewater, Gill. II. Title.
TT197.B798 1998
    684.1'6—dc21   97-51569
                                       CIP

Editor: Rodman Pilgrim Neumann

1 3 5 7 9 10 8 6 4 2
Published by Sterling Publishing Company, Inc.
387 Park Avenue South, New York, N.Y. 10016
© 1998 by Alan & Gill Bridgewater
Distributed in Canada by Sterling Publishing
c/o Canadian Manda Group, One Atlantic Avenue, Suite 105
Toronto, Ontario, Canada M6K 3E7
Distributed in Great Britain and Europe by Cassell PLC
Wellington House, 125 Strand, London WC2R 0BB, England
Distributed in Australia by Capricorn Link (Australia) Pty Ltd.
P.O. Box 6651, Baulkham Hills, Business Centre, NSW 2153, Australia
Manufactured in the United States of America
All rights reserved

Sterling ISBN 0-8069-1335-5

Contents

〜

Color section follows page 64.

Preface

"The art is in the detail"

I think we'd better start by proudly declaring that this is the only book that we have seen on making handles, hinges, latches, and catches in wood. How's that for a boast?

Every woodworker eventually runs into trouble when it comes to finding quality fixtures. I'm sure you know what I mean. The box, door, drawer, or cabinet is done, and you have put your heart and soul into the work, but, when you come to search out suitable fixtures, you find that they either don't exist or, if they do, then they are so poor-grade that they couldn't be used anyway. It happens every time! When we come to buy the hinges, and the knobs, and all the rest, we are presented with gaudy, badly designed, wretchedly made shoddy items that wouldn't do justice to the poorest of poor nail-split-and-splinter crate constructions.

Well, there we were one day, once again annoyed that we couldn't obtain a suitable latch for a beautiful oak cupboard that had been five long weeks in the making, when we realized we could make the latch from wood, and better yet, we could make everything—the latch, the catch, the handle, and the hinges!

The more we thought about it, the more logical it seemed. If we were going to make a piece of fine woodwork, and if we were going to spend hundreds of hours doing our very best to make sure that every joint, surface, and decorative detail was taken to a fine finish, then why even consider fitting second-rate metal hinges, or nasty plastic handles when we could make quality fixtures in wood?

Once we looked at the idea, then we came to see that it was not so much a question of could we make the fittings and fixtures in wood? but rather, should we ever consider doing anything else? Once the make-everything-from-wood philosophy had taken hold, we saw that our way of thinking was part of a ong tradition. For example, when the settlers wanted a door handle for their log cabin, they simply cut a crotch from a tree and built a pin-string-and-pivot handle from wood. And then again, when the Shakers came to build their cabinets, they didn't screw on an ugly shop-bought fixture. No way! They took the design problem through to its conclusion and made their own pulls and handles from wood. And so it was with the great furniture-makers like William Morris, Gustav Stickley, Charles Rennie Mackintosh, Frank Lloyd Wright—they made just about everything that went into the design. In fact, some of these designers even designed their own tools, mixed paint, tanned hide, whittled dowels, and wove upholstery!

Making Wood Handles, Hinges & Knobs is about taking total control and making everything from wood. Through the medium of the projects we take you through all the procedures: We discuss the pros and cons of the design, we talk about the qualities of the wood, we list the tools and describe how they are best used, and we discuss techniques such as fretting, laminating, bending, whittling, sculpting, shaping, and turning. With every project there are working drawings, a series of process photographs, a numbered blow-by-text. We also present you with loads of inspirational ideas that will keep you going through to the next millennium.

What else to say, except that if you are interested in quality woodwork, and if you are generally interested in controlling every aspect of design, then you need to make room on your bookshelf for *Making Wood Handles, Hinges & Knobs.*

Alan & Gillian Bridgewater

• Project 1 •
Laminated Bridge Handle

Before you get started, have a look at the project pictures and the working drawings on page eight and note how the finished handle measures a little over 4 1/2 inches in total length, about 5/8 inch across the width of the "pad," with the bridge height being about 3/4 inch. Consider the way the lamination is made up from three layers, all the curves being restrained.

Although there are many design possibilities with a handle of this character—it could be bigger, or smaller, or made from exotic wood types, or altogether fancier—I think that primarily the success of the project has to do with the curves. If the curves are too shallow the laminations will try to flatten out, and if the curves are too full the laminations will crack across the bends.

The choice of wood is critical. It needs to be strong, straight grained, free from knots, and inherently pliable. Best go for a wood like ash, elm, or beech. Last, it's always a good idea to make more handles than you need; then you can choose the best group to suit your needs.

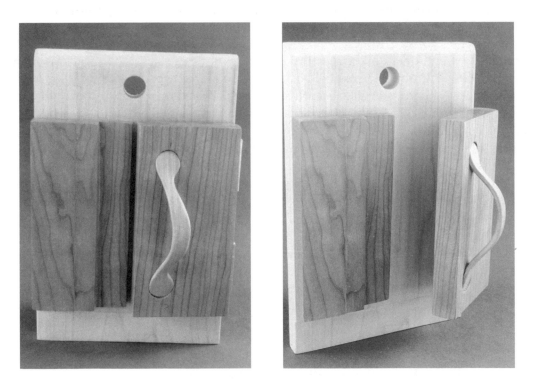

Project pictures—the finished project.

WOOD LIST

- A 7-inch length of 1 1/4-inch-thick wood at about 2 1/2 inches wide for the former or pattern block
- Three 10-inch lengths of 1/16-inch-thick wood at about 1 1/4 inch wide for each handle that you want to make

TOOLS & MATERIALS

- A small band saw or a large scroll saw
- A small hand plane
- A hand fret or coping saw
- A bird's-mouth cutting board to be used with the saw
- A pencil, ruler, and a pair of dividers
- A good sharp knife for tidying up the curves—we use a Swedish sloyd knife
- A sheet each of work-out and tracing paper
- A small fine-toothed riffler file
- A roll of 2-inch-wide double-sided carpet tape—the type that has a waxed-paper cover strip
- A roll of 1-inch-wide masking tape
- A good number of small-size clamps
- All the usual workshop tools and materials . . . sandpaper, PVA glue, dividers, scissors, etc.

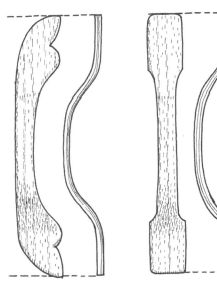

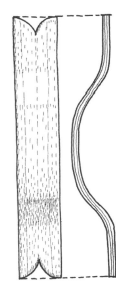

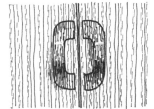

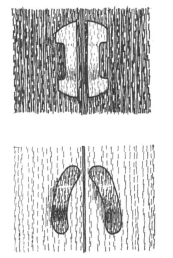

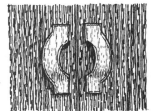

Inspirational designs. (Top) Three alternatives as seen in front and side view. (Bottom) Consider how various pairs of handles might be set together in a mirror-image arrangement to achieve a more dynamic total design.

CONSTRUCTION STAGES

Making and Preparing the Former

1. Having first studied the working drawings and carefully selected your wood, draw the "bridge" design up to full size and make a tracing.

2. Press-transfer the "bridge" design through to the wide face of your pattern wood.

3. Thicken the bridge line up until it is a uniform width of about 3/16 inch.

4. Having established the shape of the "bridge" with a clean-curved 3/16-inch-wide line—like a ribbon—cut it out on the band saw so that the strip is wasted (*see* 1-1).

5. When you are happy with the sawn faces of the bridge line, carefully cover them with the 2-inch-wide tape, so that the wood is hidden from view (*see* 1-2).

Working drawings—at a grid scale of four squares to an inch.
(Top) The pattern block.
(Bottom left) The shape of the handle as seen in side view.
(Bottom middle) The shape of the handle as seen front-on.
(Bottom right) The slightly longer shape of the handle as set out on the masking tape pattern.

LAMINATING

6. Take your three 1/16-inch-thick strips of wood—all planed to size and rubbed down—and sandwich them so that the best faces are outermost. Pencil-label the mating faces.

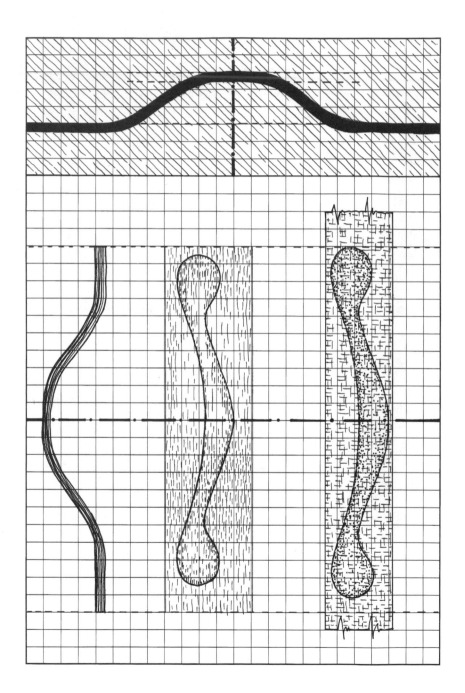

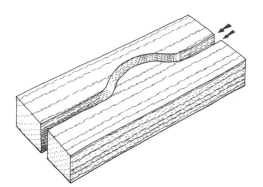

1-1 *Cut away the 3/16-inch-wide strip of waste from the two blocks so as to make the bridge-shaped pattern.*

7. Have a trial clamp-up—to see how the wood responds. By this, we mean set the strips of wood in the bridge pattern and very gently clamp until the strips conform to the pattern. If one or other of them cracks or splits, then replace it and repeat the procedure.

8. When you have achieved a successful dry run, then smear the PVA glue on all four of the mating faces and clamp up (*see* 1-3). Use as many clamps as space allows. Note that we have left off two clamps so that you can see what's going on.

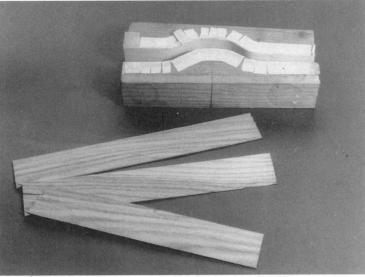

1-2 *Cover the mating surfaces with tape—either waxed paper or plastic—so that they resist the glue. If you are a really messy worker, then it might be just as well to paint the whole block with wax.*

SPECIAL TIP
We got our strips gratis from a small local joiner—they were off-cut slivers. That said, you could use thick veneers or even hand-sawn slices cut from the edge of a board.

1-3 *Smear the strips with glue, set them in the clamp, and then clamp up. Apply the pressure gradually from the center of the bridge outwards.*

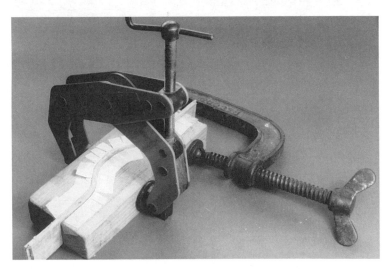

CUTTING OUT THE PROFILE & FINISHING

9. When the glue has cured, then undo the clamps and gently ease the lamination out of the pattern. Repeat the whole sequence as described, until you have the required number of "bridges." Make one or two spares for good measure—just in case you make a mess-up (*see* 1-4).

10. Trace off the shape of the handle profile and press-transfer the traced lines through to a strip of masking tape (*refer to* the bottom right of the working drawings). Repeat this procedure so that you have a separate masking tape pattern for each handle that you want to make. Note how the pattern profile is slightly longer, so as to allow for the take-up that occurs when the tape is run over the curved bridge.

11. Keeping in mind that the straight edge of the tape needs to be aligned with the side of the lamination, set the masking tape pattern in place on the topmost face of the bridge (*see* 1-5).

12. Use the coping saw and the bird's-mouth cutting board to fret out the shape of the handle profile. The best procedure is to hold and locate the workpiece so that it is as near as possible to

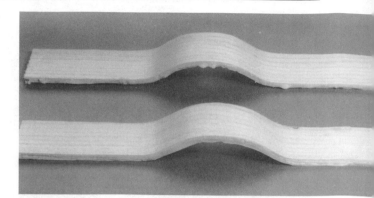

1-4 Check the finished bridges over for potentially troublesome cracks and delaminations. Don't forget to make a couple of extra bridges—just in case you mess up!

the vertex of the V, and then work from above with a series of very small light strokes. Aim to cut a little to the waste side of the drawn line (*see* 1-6).

13. When you have achieved the basic cutout, then you can use the knife, the riffler file, and the graded sandpapers to sculpt and rub the handle down to a smooth, slightly round-edged finish.

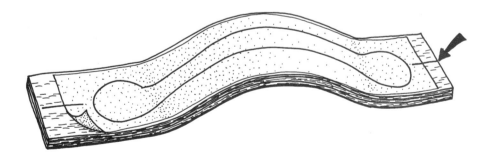

1-5 Set the masking tape pattern down on the bridge so that the center and edge lines are correctly aligned.

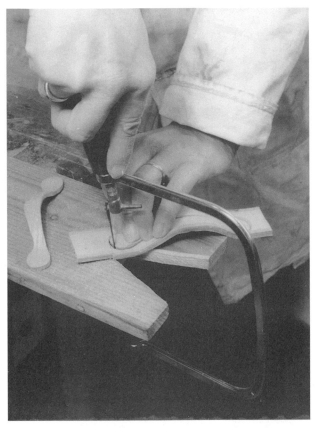

1-6 You will find that the nearer you cut to the vertex of the "V," the easier it is to achieve a clean edge.

14. Finally, wipe away the dust, give the handle a swift wipe-over with Danish oil, let it dry, and then use beeswax to burnish the surface to a dull sheen finish.

AFTERTHOUGHTS

• If you like the project but want to go for a more complex handle—perhaps bigger, with more generous curves—then it is most important that you make a swift prototype. All you need do is cut the bridge pattern and then see if the wood strips can be clamped up without splitting.

• If you do want to make a series of prototype handles, then it's a good idea to use Super Glue to bond the layers. If you work in this way you can achieve a whole heap of trials in a single day.

• When we ran a series of trials, we found that the soak time of the glue was critical—that is, the time allowed between smearing the glue on the wood and clamping up. The best procedure is to lay on the glue, let it soak in, lay on another coat, and then clamp up.

• We found that from one wood to another there is a huge difference in the way the wood behaves. This being so, it's best to run trials if you want to use exotic wood types.

• If you have in mind to make a lot of fretwork handles, then it's a good idea to smooth out the operation by working on a much narrower bird's-mouth cutting board—one that has been modified so that the projections fit the bridges.

• If you have to cut your own strips, then it's best to use a band saw to cut them from the edge of a thick board, and a sanding block to rub them down to a good, smooth finish.

• Project 2 •

Pierced & Sculpted Hole Handle

Before you put tool to wood, have a look at the project pictures below and the working drawings on page 14. This project requires the use of three large-size Forstner bits. You need a 2 1/8-inch-diameter bit for the hole in the door, a 2-inch-diameter bit for the secondary sinking, and a 1-inch-diameter bit for the sculpted hole.

Note how although the finished handle is in essence no more than a disk that is set into a stepped hole—like a lid—it is a handle that is both subtle in form and specific in its usage. This is one of those projects that is more difficult than it looks: You have to go for the right wood, you have to enjoy sculpting, and you have to be able to work to tight limits.

Having played around with the notion of creating handles by cutting circle and part-circle inserts that can be fitted lid-like into a drilled hole, we see that there are hundreds of exciting design possibilities. While you are looking at the page of inspirational ideas, note how it is possible to extend the disk handle theme so that the counterchange between the handle and its siting becomes a primary design feature.

Project pictures—the finished project.

As with so many of the projects, the choice of wood is most important. It's all the more so with this undertaking, because of its small size and relatively slender form, and simply because the wood needs to be sculpted. It's essential that the disk be made from a wood that is strong, tight grained, easy-to-carve, and decorative. That said, although we decided to use a piece of English plum, you could just as well use a species like cherry, box, beech, or yew. If you have doubts, then ask the advice of a specialist at your supplier.

WOOD LIST
- A 1/4-inch-thick off-cut of wood at about 2 1/2 x 2 1/2 inches square for each handle that you want to make

TOOLS & MATERIALS
- An electric scroll saw
- A bench drill press
- Forstner drill bits in the sizes 2 1/8 inches, 2 inches, and 1 inch diameter
- A small, shallow sweep gouge
- A miniature power tool sander— we use a Foredom Micro Motor carving system
- A pencil, ruler, and a pair of dividers
- A good sharp knife for tidying up the curves—we use a Swedish sloyd knife
- A sheet each of work-out and tracing paper
- A small, fine-toothed riffler file
- All the usual workshop tools and materials . . . sandpaper, PVA glue, dividers, scissors, etc.

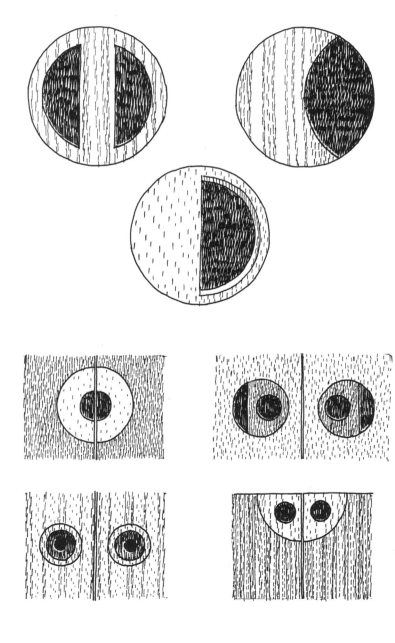

Inspirational designs.
(Top) Three alternatives as seen in front view.
(Bottom) Four designs showing how the sculpted circle idea can be used to create a dynamic design feature.

CONSTRUCTION STAGES

Drilling the Holes & Marking Out

1. Having first decided where you want the handle to be located—it might be on a door, drawer, or wherever—have a good long look at the working drawing and consider how the design of the handle needs to be sited in wood that is at least 3/4 inch thick. Or, to put it another way, if your cupboard is framed up and hollow, or made from particleboard, or less than 3/4 inch thick, then you need to sit down and maybe reconsider what you are doing.

2. When you have a clear understanding as to where and how the handle is to be placed, take your 1/4-inch-thick piece of choice wood to the drill press and use the 2 1/8-inch-diameter Forstner bit to scribe out the primary circle that goes to make up the design (see 2-1). Don't go too deep—only until the outside edge cutter part of the bit makes its mark. Be sure to set the circle on the most interesting area of grain.

3. With the handle marked out with a scribed circle, take the pencil and ruler and run a guideline through the center point.

4. Allowing for a 1/8-inch bridge of wood between the edge of the 1-inch-diameter hole and the scribed line (see 2-2), fit the drill press with the 1-inch bit, center it on the guideline, and drill a single hole through the wood.

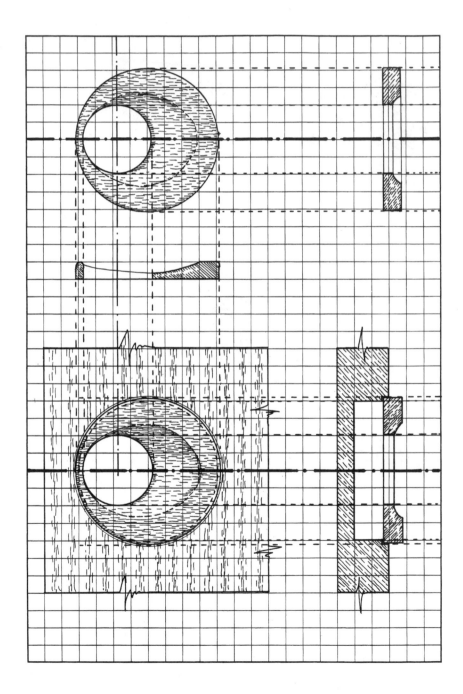

Working drawing—at a grid scale of four squares to an inch.
Have a good long look at the section detail at bottom right, and see how the disk is fitted lid-like, being stepped.

2-1 (Left)
Use the 2 1/8-inch-diameter Forstner bit to scribe out the basic circle.

2-2 (Right)
Run the 1-inch-diameter hole right through the thickness of the wood.

FRETTING & SCULPTING

5. Take the workpiece to the scroll saw and very carefully fret out the 2 1/8-inch-diameter disk. Be warned, there is little or no leeway for mistakes. If you run over the line then you will have to start over—so work at a nice easy pace. Make sure that the line of cut is slightly to the waste side of the scribed line (*see* 2-3).

6. Flip the disk over so that its best side is down; then take your small gouge and set to work dishing out the back. Work with small, tight, controlled strokes, all the while cutting from the outer edge through to the hole (*see* 2-4). Aim to start the cuts about 1/8 inch in from the edge of the disk.

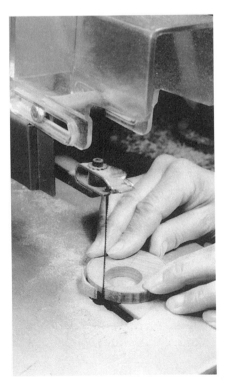

SPECIAL TIP
For optimum control, you could work with the disk set in a recess; then you would be able to do the sculpting without undue risk to your fingers.

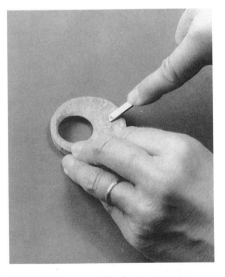

2-3 (Left) Use the scroll saw to fret out the circle shape. Note how our use of a slack blunt blade resulted in a burnt-edge cut.

2-4 Use a small-size gouge to lower the waste at the back of the disk. Be careful that you don't slip and do damage to your fingers and/or the workpiece.

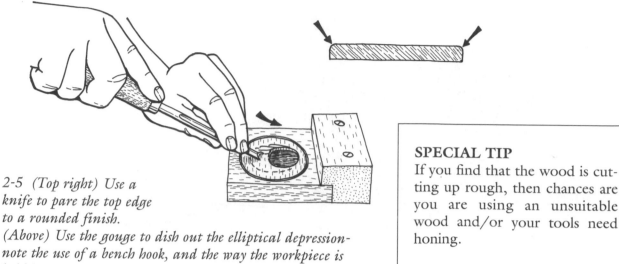

2-5 (Top right) Use a
knife to pare the top edge
to a rounded finish.
(Above) Use the gouge to dish out the elliptical depression—
note the use of a bench hook, and the way the workpiece is
held in a piece of waste wood.

SPECIAL TIP
If you find that the wood is cutting up rough, then chances are you are using an unsuitable wood and/or your tools need honing.

7. When you have dished out the back—to the extent that the rim of the finger hole has been reduced to a thickness of about 1/8 inch—then turn the disk so that its best side is uppermost and use the gouge and the knife to sculpt the edge and to dish the area around the hole (*see* 2-5). Aim for an edge that is slightly rounded and an oval-shaped dished area that encompasses the hole.

8. Having worked the disk with the knife and gouge, then comes the tricky task of sanding the whole works to a good finish. I say tricky, because it's all too easy to overdo the sanding to the extent that the disk is a sloppy, loose fit. This being so, it's a good idea to run a 2 1/8-inch-diameter hole into a piece of rough wood, and then to repeat trial fittings throughout the sanding procedure.

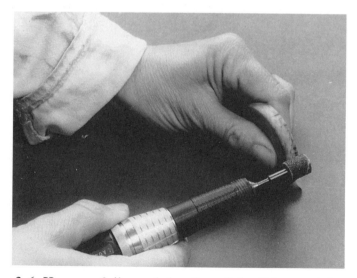

2-6 Very carefully sand the edges of the disk to a tight push-fit.

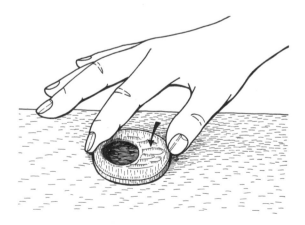

2-7 The only way to achieve a good fit is to sand a little, have a fitting, note where the area needs reducing, and then sand a little more, and so on.

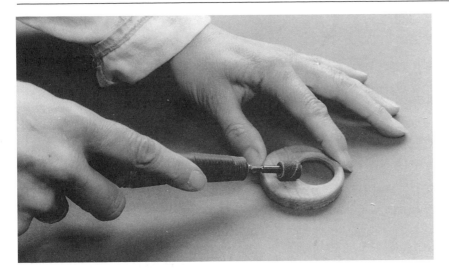

When you come to drilling the stepped recess in your workpiece—that is, in your door or drawer front or whatever—it is of course essential that you sink the 2 1/8-inch hole first and then follow up with the 2-inch hole. You can't do it the other way around!

2-8 *Use the little drum sander to bring the face of the wood to a good finish.*

9. With the little size-test rig at the ready, take the power sander—or you might use a piece of sandpaper and a lot of elbow grease—and sand the edges to achieve a good fit (*see* 2-6 and 2-7).

10. When you have achieved a tight push-fit, then use a mix of the power tool and the hand sanding to rub the face of the disk to a smooth finish (*see* 2-8).

11. Finally, glue the turning in place in the recess.

AFTERTHOUGHTS

- If you like the notion of this project but are not comfortable with large-size Forstner drill bits—or any drill bits—then it is possible to cut the holes with a mallet and gouge. And then again, you could change the shape of the handle and go for a free-form hole, or even a straight-sided form.
- The choice of wood is all-important—you must use a tight-grained wood that is free from splits and knots.

• Project 3 •

Pierced Arts & Crafts Handle

Of all the projects in the book, the Arts & Crafts handle is a bit of a contradiction in that it is one of the most basic, one of the easiest to do, one of the trickiest, and one of the most sophisticated. It's basic because it can be managed with the simplest of tools—just a scroll saw and a knife. It's easy because, after all, it is no more than a couple of holes. It's tricky because there is no room for mistakes; and it's sophisticated because the various lines that go to make up the design need to be carefully considered in relationship to one another. Okay, so the handle is only made up from two holes, but then again these two holes do have to be fretted out with a considerable degree of care and precision. Have a look at the project pictures and the working drawings.

Having studied all manner of Arts & Crafts details—drawer fronts, bed boards, cupboard doors, and such like—we see that there are many design possibilities that have to do with cutting holes. Basically the holes can be organized in two ways. They can be worked as single holes—in which case the hole itself is the handle—or the holes can be used in pairs (as in this project), in

Project pictures—the finished project.

which case the bridge of wood between the two holes becomes the handle. The only other thing that needs saying—and this is pretty obvious but very important if you have spent hundreds of hours making a piece of furniture—is that the holes are cut directly in the front of your piece of furniture. This means in the door, or drawer, or whatever. Or, to put it another way, if you make a mess-up with this project, then you mess up a whole door frame, or a whole drawer front!

WOOD LIST
- A piece of furniture that requires a pierced handle. (Note that if you don't want the holes to be left open, then you will need to use a backing piece as shown.)

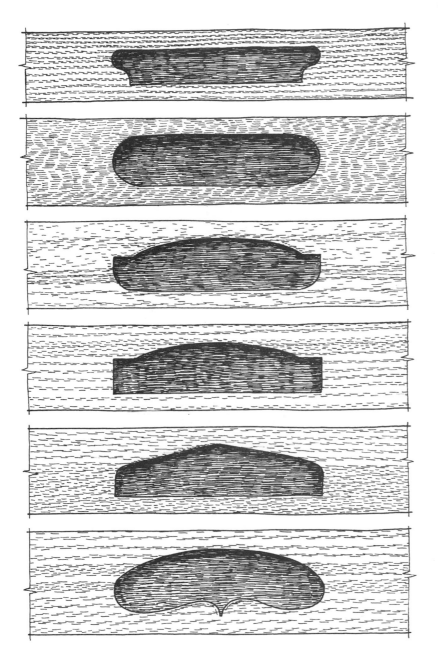

TOOLS & MATERIALS
- An electric scroll saw
- A bench drill press with a Forstner bit at about 1/4–3/8 inch
- A pencil, ruler, and a pair of dividers
- A selection of good sharp knives for whittling and for tidying up the curves—we use a Swedish sloyd knife—and a couple of small penknives
- A sheet each of work-out and tracing paper
- A spray can of fixative—the kind used to prevent pencil and pastel drawings from smudging
- All the usual workshop tools and materials . . . sandpaper, PVA glue, dividers, scissors, etc.

Inspirational designs.
Six alternative profiles that can be used as simple hole handles or paired to make bridge handles.

CONSTRUCTION STAGES

Marking Out

1. Having first decided where you want the handle to be located—it might be on a door, drawer, or wherever—take a good long look at the working drawing and consider how you might want to modify the design by regrouping the holes. Draw the design up to full size and make a tracing.

2. Keeping in mind that you might well mess up the first time around, it's a good idea to have a tryout on a piece of scrap wood. Select one of your end-of-board off-cuts and check it over to make certain that it is free from splits.

3. Set your chosen piece of wood out with two center-lines that cross at right angles to each other—one running in line with the grain and one running across the grain.

4. Align the tracing with the centerlines, attach it in place with tabs of masking tape, and carefully pencil-press-transfer the lines of the design through to the wood. Remove the tracing paper and shade in the areas that need to be cut away (*see* **3-1**).

5. When you have sharpened and cleaned up the design and generally made sure that every single line is well placed, spray the whole works with the fixative and put it to one side to dry.

Working drawings—at a grid scale of four squares to an inch. Note especially the detail at bottom right that shows the handle in cross section.

SPECIAL TIP

The handle does of course have to be aligned with the grain, for the plain and simple reason that if the "bridge" is to be strong, then the grain must run along its length. Choose your wood with great care—no knots or ragged grain—just nice, clean, close-grain hardwood. We have gone for a piece of English plum, but you might also use a species like American cherry, European box, English beech, maple, or yew. If you need help, then you'd best ask the advice of a local specialist supplier.

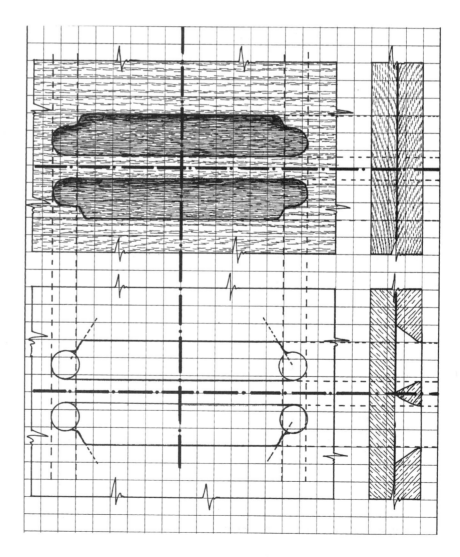

DRILLING PILOT HOLES & FRETTING OUT

6. Having first backed the workpiece with a piece of scrap wood—so as to prevent damage when the drill bit exits—move to the drill press and very carefully run a hole through each of the "windows" that needs to be cut away. Go at it nice and slowly, all the while being wary that you don't damage the wood.

7. With the holes in place, spend time making sure that your scroll/fret saw is in good working order, check that you have a good supply of fine blades . . . and then to work.

8. The working procedure for cutting the "windows" is:

- Release the tension and unhitch the top end of the blade.
- Pass the blade through the pilot hole and refit and re-tension.
- Switch on the power and set to work running the line of cut slightly to the waste side of the drawn line.
- Don't rush, don't force the pace, and don't let the workpiece vibrate intensely.

SPECIAL TIP

Although on the face of it, drilling holes doesn't seem to be much of a problem, many beginners are apt to be so blasé about the whole procedure that they fall at the first hurdle. The secret of success is to go at it slowly, and to use the best bits for the job. In the context of boring medium-size holes in cabinetry, we invariably use Forstner bits for the simple reason that they produce clean-sided holes with the minimum of face damage.

9. When you have achieved the first hole (*see* 3-2), then unhitch the blade and repeat the whole procedure for the second. It's all easy enough, as long as you take your time, and as long as you make sure that the two holes are nicely aligned so that the "bridge" is the same width along its length.

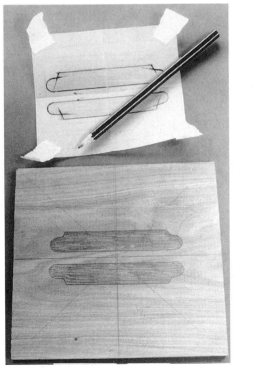

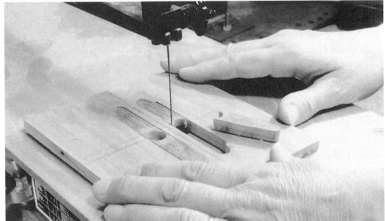

3-1 (Left) Having used tabs of masking tape to ensure that the tracing stays put, and reworked the transferred lines with a pencil and ruler, then shade in the area that needs to be cut away.

3-2 (Above) Run the line of cut slightly to the waste side of the drawn line. Bear in mind that if you do make a slip-up, then it must occur in the waste. There is little room for error.

WHITTLING & SHAPING THE CHAMFERS

10. If you start by looking at the bottom right of the working drawings, you will notice that the underside edges of the pierced holes need to be chamfered so that the bridge handle is more or less triangular in cross section. The important thing to note here is that while the underside needs to be chamfered and undercut, the profile outline on the front face must remain untouched. If the front edge of the hole gets to be nicked or cut, then the success of the project is put at risk.

11. When you have a clear understanding of the best way forward, pencil-label the back face of the workpiece, hone your knives . . . and then to work.

12. Run a centerline down the length of the bridge handle, and a line about 3/8 inch in from the edge of the hole; then take your biggest knife—we use the Swedish sloyd knife—and clear away the angle of waste and establish the basic chamfer. Not forgetting that you must never cut directly into the end grain, work with a tight paring grip (*see* 3-3).

SPECIAL TIP
The thickness of the chamfered edge will, to a great extent, reflect your choice of wood. For example, while you can whittle plum and American cherry down to a slender edge of 1/16 inch, you couldn't do the same with a loose-grained mahogany or a stringy pine. Either way, be mindful that the bridge handle is going to get a fair amount of wear.

13. And so you continue, working around and around the holes, until you reach the guidelines. Keep working until the angled chamfers on each side of the bridge handle meet the centerline.

14. Take your smallest knives, and scrape and trim back the chamfers. Carefully continue trimming and scraping the chamfered edge so that the wood thickness—as seen through the holes from the front face—is reduced to about 1/16 inch (*see* 3-4).

3-3 (Left) Cut with the run of the grain—that is, from the end through to the center.

3-4 (Right) Use a small knife to skim the chamfer to a good finish. Hold the knife like a scraper—so that the edge of the blade is more or less at right angles to the surface of the wood.

15. Finally, when you are pleased with your efforts, use the fine-grade sandpaper to rub the whole works down to a smooth finish, fit and attach the workpiece to the item of furniture. Then burnish to a good finish with beeswax polish.

AFTERTHOUGHTS

- If you like the notion of this project but can't get to use a pillar drill or a Forstner drill bit, or even an electric scroll saw, don't despair. You can use a hand drill, twist bits, and a hand coping saw fitted with a fine blade. Certainly there will be a lot more sweat, but then again, the slow hand-sawing may well be the best way forward for you.

- It needs emphasizing that the choice of wood is all-important. Don't make the classic beginner's mistake of having a practice dry run with poor-grade wood. If you do, then you may well get discouraged and not move on to better things.

- You might think that a knife is a knife and any knife will do just fine—but not a bit of it! You need to use a knife that is capable of holding a keen edge. If in doubt, then we recommend a Swedish sloyd knife—one that has a laminated-steel blade.

• Project 4 •

Chinese Calligraphy Handle

Have a good long look at the project pictures, the inspirational designs, and the working drawings and note how this project draws its inspirational from Chinese ideograms or written characters. It's not that we know anything at all about Chinese calligraphy, it's just that when we came to look at the brush stroke shapes, we immediately thought about how they could be interpreted as handles.

This is essentially a fairly low-tech project, inasmuch as you don't need many more tools than a bow or coping saw, a knife, and a couple of drill bits.

If you study the inspirational designs you will see that, in essence, this type of handle has one or two doweled-tenon supports, one or more through-bars, the whole structure being held together with little pins or pegs. The exciting thing about this project is the way that the structure and the fixings are all up-front and visible.

The choice of wood is all the more important in this project in that not only does it need to be easy to carve and tight grained, it must be more or less free from knots and split resistant. And of course you need to use contrasting colors. We chose English plum for the two crotch pieces,

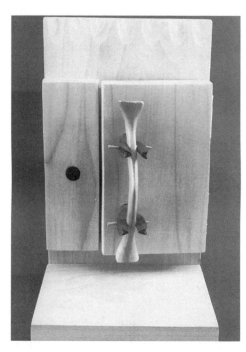 

Project pictures—the finished project.

English lime for the cross bar, and European boxwood for the fixing pins. You could also go for species like cherry, beech, yew, maple, pear, and sycamore.

WOOD LIST
- A 6-inch length of lime at 1 1/2 x 2 inches in cross section
- A couple of 3-inch-long off-cuts of plum at about 1/2 inch thick and 1 1/4 inches wide
- A couple of slivers of boxwood for the pins

SPECIAL TIP
Don't be tempted to try this project with a bit of rough knotty pine or ragged oak or some such—it will only cause you grief. Certainly some choice woods are expensive, but then again, some specialist suppliers will be glad to give you off-cuts free.

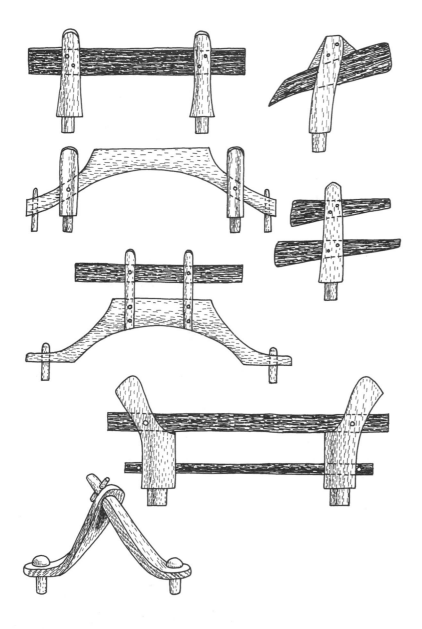

TOOLS & MATERIALS
- A coping or bow saw
- A bench drill press
- Forstner drill bits in the sizes 3/8 inch and 1/8 inch diameter
- A small hand drill
- A small, shallow sweep gouge
- A pencil, ruler, and a pair of dividers
- A good sharp knife for whittling—we use a Swedish sloyd knife
- A sheet each of work-out and tracing paper
- All the usual workshop tools and materials . . . sandpaper, PVA glue, dividers, scissors, etc.

Inspirational designs.
All the designs draw their inspiration from Chinese calligraphy forms.

CONSTRUCTION STAGES

Cutting the Blank

1. Having first selected your three wood types, and studied the working drawings, and generally considered how you want the design to be, then draw the bridge part of the handle up to size and make clear tracings. Staying with the bridge analogy, you need two views: one showing the bridge side-on, and the other as seen from above.

2. Take your chosen 6-inch length of wood and pencil-press the traced views through to the appropriate faces. Don't worry too much about trying to achieve a precise image; just go for the broad form.

3. When you are happy with the drawn profiles, take your saw and cut the bridge shape out as seen in side view (*see* 4-1). Once again, don't fret about trying to have the cut dead-on; just make sure that it runs to the waste side of the drawn line.

4. Use masking tape to strap the cut-away pieces back together. Take care not to cover the bridge with pieces of tape so that you still can see the drawn guidelines. With the pieces secured, saw the shape out, as seen in bird's-eye view. The cutout can be quite free, but you should finish up with a sort of elongated asymmetrical bow-tie form (*see* 4-2).

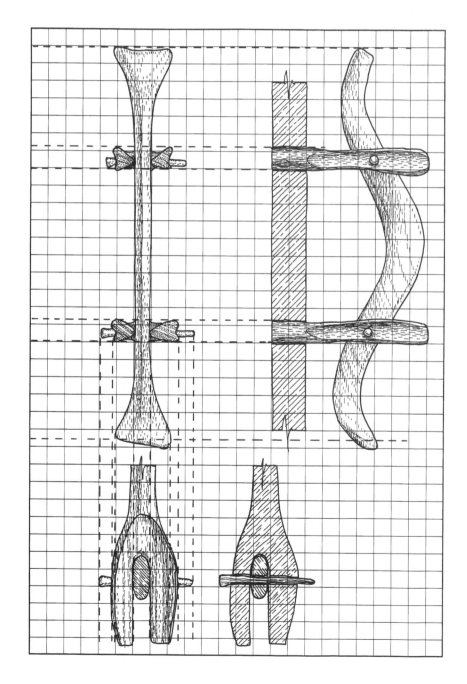

Working drawings—at a grid scale of four squares to an inch.

Note especially the top view of the crotch—as enclosed in the circle. Consider how the two heart-shaped prongs appear to nip the bridge handle.

4-1 Fret out the bridge blank—as seen in side view.

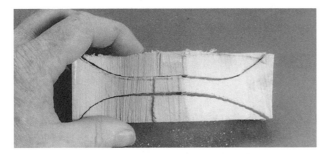

4-2 Fret out the bridge—as seen in plan view. Note how the cutout can be quite free and asymmetrical.

WHITTLING THE BRIDGE & THE CROTCHES

5. Keeping in mind that the bridge shape has end grain showing on all the long faces and fragile short-grain areas at the ends, take the knife and swiftly go over the wood, skimming off the sharp corners and edges (*see* 4-3).

6. Although it is pretty easy to whittle the shape, you do have to watch out that you cut in the correct direction to the grain—or to put it another way, you must be careful that you don't split the wood by running the knife into end grain (*see* 4-4).

SPECIAL TIP
Whittling is easy if you work with a good knife. If you enjoy whittling, you could start a knife collection. Little pre-war knives are usually a good bet—especially penknives and pruning knives.

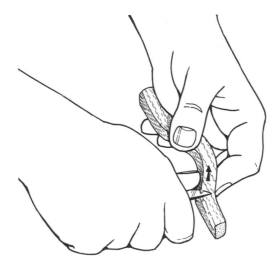

4-3 For optimum control, do the whittling with a tightly braced thumb-paring stroke. Note how the direction of the cuts relates to the run of the grain.

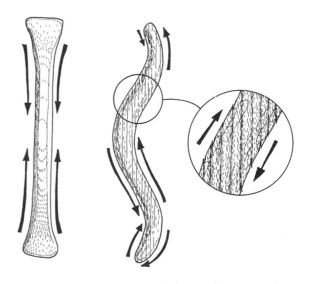

4-4 If you always cut with the grain—meaning in the direction of the arrows—then you will avoid running the blade into end grain and splitting the wood.

7. And so you continue whittling, until the bridge shape begins to take on what you consider is a pleasing form. And of course if you fancy that the form needs to be thinner or slightly more curved, then now is the time to make modifications. For example, when we came to the fragile short-grain end corners, we decided to have done with the fiddling and fussing about and slice them off (*see* 4-5).

8. When you have achieved a pleasing bridge shape, take the two pieces of wood that you have chosen for the supports and swiftly cut them down with the saw so that they are slotted to fit the bridge (*see* 4-6). Be mindful that the bridge-in-slot needs to be a tight push-fit.

9. Now is the time to make a little test-fitting jig. Take a short length of scrap wood—about 6 inches long and 1/2 inch thick will do just fine—and drill two 3/8-inch-diameter holes. Have the holes placed so they are apart at about 2 1/2 inches between centers.

10. Still working with the knife, carefully size the stems of the crotches. Make sure that they provide a tight push-fit when positioned in the test jig holes (*see* 4-7).

11. And so you continue, whittling away at the bridge, fitting the bridge in the crotches, shaping the profile of the crotches, and so on, until all three component parts come together to make a satisfactory whole.

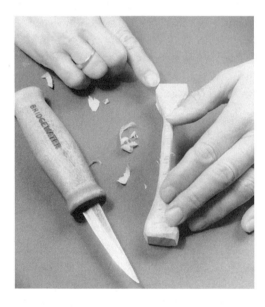

4-5 (Left) In light of the fact that the short-grain corners kept crumbling away, we decided to cut them off at an angle and go for a more rounded form.

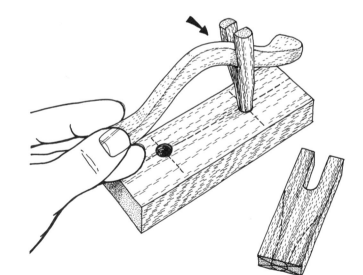

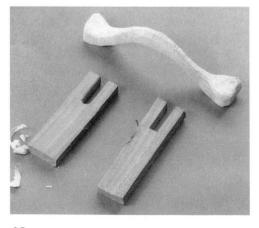

4-6 (Left) Make sure that the slots are sized so that the bridge shape is a tight push-fit. Shape the bottom of the slots to fit the section of the handle.

4-7 (Above) Have repeated trial fittings along the way—until the bridge fits the crotches and the crotches fit the holes. Pencil-label the components so that you know what goes where.

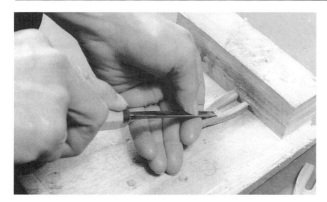

4-8 *Use a restrained two-hand cut—one pushing and the other guiding and maneuvering.*

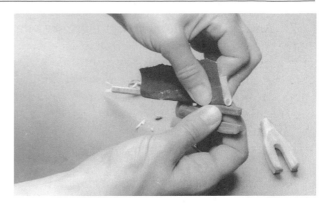

4-9 *Sand a little runnel around the sides and over the top of each prong.*

FINISHING

12. When you have completed the overall handle unit, then comes the very pleasurable task of fine-modeling the details. Having decided that the bridge shape looked very bone-like, we decided to stay with this theme and hollow-carve the surfaces of the crotches so that they would take on a bone-like quality.

13. To model the crotches, butt them flat down against a bench hook—so that the two prongs are looking away from you. Then take the small gouge and gently hollow out the face of the "Y" so as to achieve a "U"-shaped depression (*see* 4-8). Do this on both sides of both crotches.

14. When you are satisfied with the front face, wrap a fold of fine-grade sandpaper around a piece of 1/4-inch-diameter dowel and gently rub the sides of the crotches down so that they are also concave in section (*see* 4-9).

15. Now, having first looked at the working drawing details again, notice that the crotches are shown in the top left view. Especially note how the prongs are heart shaped in cross section, and then use the knife and the sandpaper to bring the details to completion.

16. Fit the three components together, set them in the test jig, and use the hand drill to run 1/8-inch-diameter holes through the side of the crotch—so that the handle is held fast with a through-pin or peg. Be very careful to align the drill so that the bit enters and exits on line.

17. Finally, whittle the two boxwood pegs to a tight push-fit, give the whole works a burnish with beeswax, and the handle is finished.

AFTERTHOUGHTS

- If you are finding the whittling rough going, then you may be working with the wrong type of knife. Your knife doesn't have to be new or expensive—but it does have to be sharp. Swedish laminated-steel sloyd knives are inexpensive and hold a good edge. You could take an old kitchen knife and grind and hone it to shape. It's the type and quality of the blade—meaning the steel—that dictates whether or not the knife is suitable.
- If your wood is cutting up rough even though you are working with a good knife, then your wood is likely to be damp and it may have twisted grain and knots.

• Project 5 •
Turned Knob & Pin Handle

Appraise the project pictures and the working drawings, and note how this project primarily requires the use of a lathe fitted with a chuck. Consider how the success of the handle has to do with the rough-smooth relationship between the crisply turned knob and the swiftly whittled through-pin.

Having experimented with the idea of creating handles by having a main knob and a through-pin, we see that there are many possibilities—everything from turned knobs with turned pins, to pairs of knobs with a bar that makes a pull handle.

As with all the projects, the choice of wood is most important. We decided to use boxwood throughout—stained black for the main knob and left plain for the pin—for the plain simple reason that it is easy to turn and dimensionally stable. Okay, so boxwood can only be obtained in relatively small pieces, and it is sometimes difficult to prepare, but for our part these negative points are more than offset by the fact that it is predictable. If you look closely at one of the photographs, you will see that our particular piece contains a hidden cavity. Fortunately the cavity turned up in an area of waste, but it could

Project pictures—the finished project.

have made for difficulties. Other good alternatives are cherry, plum, beech, pear, English sycamore, maple, lime, or yew.

As to why we decided to stain the boxwood black rather than start out with an exotic black wood like, say, ebony, it's simply that we prefer not to use endangered species, plus we're not so happy with the fine dust produced by some exotics—they make our eyes water.

WOOD LIST

- A 1 1/2 x 1 1/2-inch-square section piece of wood about 3 inches long for each handle you want to make
- A length of easy-to-carve wood at about 1/2 x 1/2 inch square for the through-pins— long enough to hold

TOOLS & MATERIALS

- A lathe fitted with a four-jaw chuck
- A bench drill press fitted with a single 1/4-inch-diameter Forstner drill bit
- A selection of woodturning tools
- A pencil and ruler
- A pair each of calipers and dividers
- A good sharp knife for whittling the pins/pegs—we use a Swedish sloyd knife
- A sheet each of work-out and tracing paper
- A permanent black felt-tip marker pen
- All the usual workshop tools and materials . . . sandpaper, PVA glue, etc.

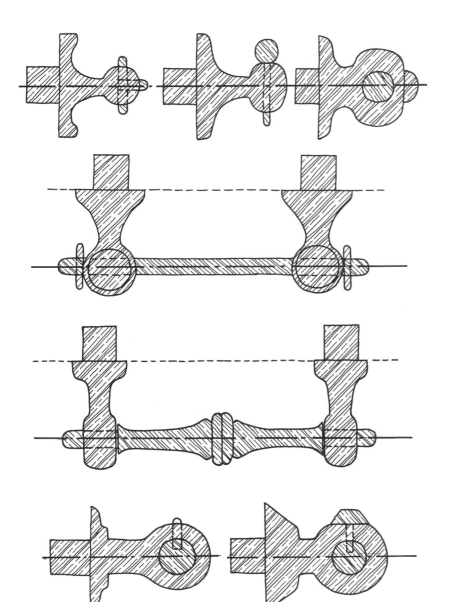

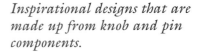

Inspirational designs that are made up from knob and pin components.

CONSTRUCTION STAGES

Roughing Out & Sinking the Waste

1. Having first made sure that your lathe is in good, safe order, take your chosen length of wood, check that it is free from splits, warps, and knots, establish the end centers, and then mount it securely on the lathe.

2. With your tools comfortably at hand, take the gouge and swiftly turn the wood to the largest possible round section (*see* 5-1).

3. Take the large skew chisel, adjust the tool rest to suit the working-on-top-of-the-wood action of the skew chisel, and then turn the wood down to a finished diameter of 1 1/4 inches.

4. When you have achieved a clean cylinder, take the dividers and work along the wood, setting out all the step-offs that go to make up the design.

5. Double-check that the step-offs are correct, then use the calipers and the parting tool to turn down the various core diameters: the central area of parting waste and the tenons at either end (*see* 5-2).

Working drawings—at a grid scale of four squares to an inch.

Note how the form needs to be precisely turned, and all the lines crisply defined. See how the swiftly carved texture of whittled pin/peg nicely balances the cool precision of the turning.

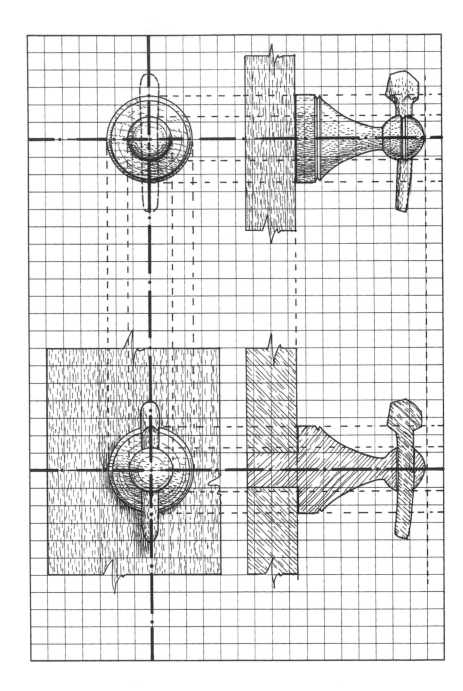

MODELING & DRILLING

6. Having first lowered the whole central area to the level of the ball heads, then use the round-nosed scraper to turn down the curves that run from the foot through to the neck (*see* 5-3). The best procedure is to shift backward and forward from form to form, all the while trying to match up the various levels and curves.

5-1 Having swiftly turned the workpiece down to a round section, stop and make sure that the wood is free from flaws.

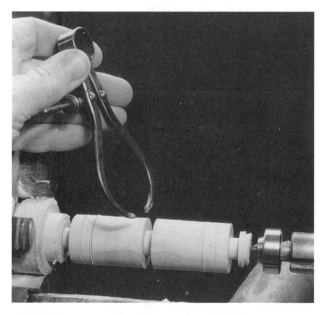

5-2 If you are a beginner, then it is best to stop the machine before taking caliper readings. Also it's best to use a pair of dividers that have a stay-put screw adjustment.

7. And so you continue to work the two forms in tandem, turning down the curve on the left-hand knob, and then the curve on the right-hand knob, and then back to the left-hand knob, and so on—all the while doing your best to match up the various elements (*see* 5-4).

SPECIAL TIP

When you are trying to make a matched pair of knobs, or cones, or whatever, it's always a good idea to arrange them so that they are set together in mirror-image fashion—either head to head or tail to tail. You will find that the symmetrical mirror-image placing of the two items will help you to weigh and access one form against another.

5-3 Turn the tenons down to your nearest drill bit size, and make sure that the ball head diameter matches the step-off length—so that you can turn a full ball. Note that the ball heads have to be set out with a centerline.

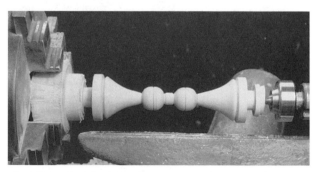

5-4 The finished knobs ready to be parted off.

8. When you have achieved what you consider are two well-matched forms, take the workpiece from the lathe and use a fine-toothed saw to part off at the center and at the ends of the tenons.

9. Push the tail stock back out of the way, secure the workpiece in the chuck, and bring the tool rest up so that you can approach the knob end-on. Check that the tenon ends are firmly gripped in the jaws.

10. Swiftly turn off the stub of waste at the ball end—you could use a round-nosed scraper or a small gouge—then use the sandpaper to rub the end-grain to a good finish (*see* 5-5).

11. Use the marker pen to blacken the surface of the wood, then take beeswax and burnish the knob to a high-shine finish. Repeat this whole procedure for both knobs.

12. Move to the drill press and spend time setting up a block of wood so that the head of the knob is supported and located in a little dip or dimple (*see* 5-6).

13. With the axis of the workpiece held parallel to the working surface, carefully run a 1/4-inch-diameter hole through the ball end at top center.

WHITTLING THE PINS

14. Take your length of 1/2 x 1/2-inch-square wood, and set it out with all the step-offs that go to make the design: 1 1/2 inches for the first pin, 1/2 inch for the first pin head, 1/4 inch for cutting waste, 1 1/2 inches for the second pin, 1/2 inch for the second pin head, and so on along the wood.

15. With the greater length of the wood pointing back under your arms, and with the first 1 1/2-inch step-off looking forward, take your knife and set to work skimming the first 1 1/2-inch length down to a rounded 1/4-inch-diameter section (*see* 5-7).

16. You will be able to tell that you are doing it correctly, because you will not only find that the wood is comfortable to hold, but better yet, the thumb-braced paring action will naturally result in a nicely curved shoulder that runs down from the head to the slender part of the pin. Continue whittling until the pin is a push-fit through the knob hole.

17. When you are happy with the first pin, carefully run a stop-cut and V-groove around the band of waste. And then nip it off from its neighbor.

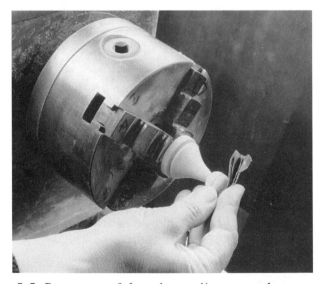

5-5 Be very careful at the sanding stage that you don't knock the workpiece off center—be very light-handed.

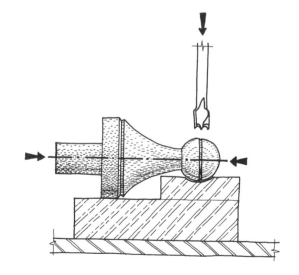

5-6 Cut a small piece of waste wood to size and use it as a support for the round head. The head needs to be resting in a slight dimple.

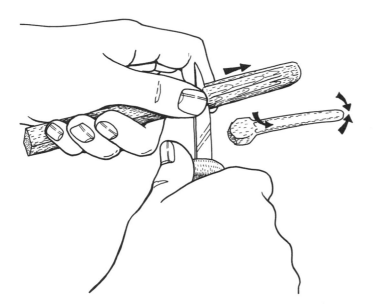

5-7 Hold the workpiece so that the greater part of the wood is under your arm, and use a thumb-braced paring action to whittle the pin to shape.

18.   Finally, whittle the head to a rough-rounded shape, slice the cheeks at either side of the head to a flat finish, round over the tail end so that it not too sharp—and the job is done. Repeat this procedure for the other pin.

AFTERTHOUGHTS

• If you like the idea of this project but can't find or can't afford boxwood, then you could just as well use a wood like maple or holly. Simply make sure that your chosen wood is free from splits and cavities.

• Be warned that we have removed the chuck guard for the photographs so that you can clearly see what's going on. On no account should you be working with an unguarded four-jaw chuck!

• Make sure that your felt-tip pen is of the permanent spirit/alcohol type—don't use water-based inks.

• Project 6 •
Beaded & Grooved Handle

Before you jump in and decide to make this handle, have a good long look at the project pictures and the working drawings, and consider how this project is made almost entirely using old wooden planes. We used a wooden plow for the groove, a wooden three-reed molding plane for the convex half-rounds, or reeds, and a simple wooden hollow molding plane for the nose of the handle. This is not to say that it's a difficult project, only that you do need the correct tools. Wooden planes can still be obtained at boot sales and flea markets for a relatively small amount of money.

The choice of wood is always important—even more so when you are using planes. Avoid wood that is rough grained, knotty, or in any way difficult to work. We decided to use American cherry throughout.

Project pictures—the finished project.

WOOD LIST

- A piece of furniture in the making—at the design stage—that has drawers
- The drawer front at 3/4 inch thick
- A strip section at 3/4 x 1 1/2 inches for the drawer pull—a length to match up with your drawer width

TOOLS & MATERIALS

- A plow plane fitted with a 3/4-inch-wide cutting iron
- A 3/4-inch-wide "hollow" molding plane
- A three-reed molding plane
- A bench fitted with a vise, a holdfast, and various stops
- A pencil and ruler
- A marking gauge
- A pair of dividers
- A good sharp knife for tidying up—we use a Swedish sloyd knife
- A sheet each of work-out and tracing paper
- All the usual workshop tools and materials . . . sandpaper, PVA glue, etc.

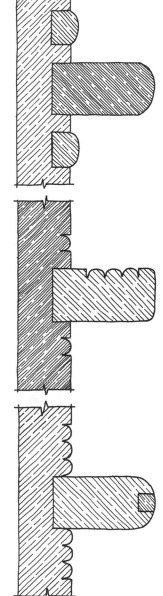

Inspirational designs that use molding plane profiles.

CONSTRUCTION STAGES

Plowing the Groove

1. Having checked your wood over to make certain that it is free from knots and splits, and generally studied the working drawings, and maybe even had a tryout with the wood and the tools, then spend time bringing your three planes to good order (*see* 6-1). Hone and polish the cutting bevels, and rub the soles and fences with candle wax.

2. Take the ready prepared drawer front, make decisions as to the best face and the best edge, and then use the pencil, ruler, and gauge to establish the precise position of the 3/4-inch-wide groove.

3. Position the workpiece so that the edge is clear of the bench and secure with the holdfast. Make sure that you can have a free run without the plow knocking into the holdfast.

4. Adjust the fence so that the cutting iron is well placed (*see* 6-2), and set the depth gauge foot at about 1/4 to 3/8 of an inch.

> **SPECIAL TIP**
> If you intend working with large-width boards, you could search the flea markets for an old wooden panel gauge. Often made in mahogany, with a stem about 24–30 inches long and a rebated fence held in place with a captive key wedge, this is the perfect tool for striking off guidelines along the lengths of boards—that is, scoring lines that are parallel with the sides.

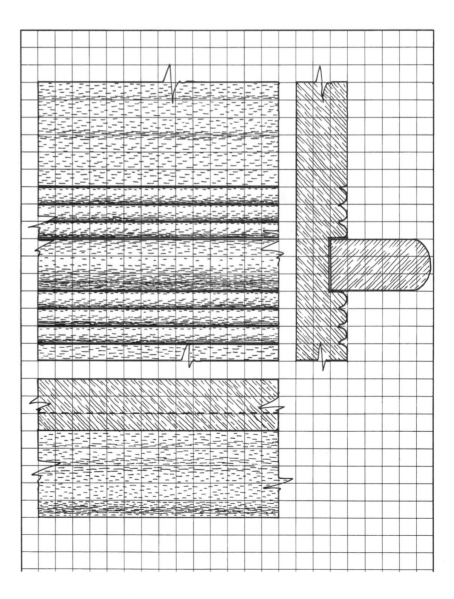

Working drawings—at a grid scale of four squares to an inch.
Note how the rounded nosing nicely reflects the round profile of the reeding.

5. Finally, having first double-checked that the cutting iron is set for a paper-thin shaving, make repeated passes until the groove is cut. It's all simple enough, as long as you start the groove from the end of the wood that is farthest away and then back up. Hold the fence hard up against the edge of the workpiece as you work the plane to form the groove.

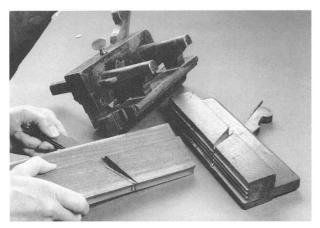

6-1 *Check that your chosen planes are in good order—with well-honed cutting irons, waxed-burnished soles, and with the fence edges/rebates undamaged.*

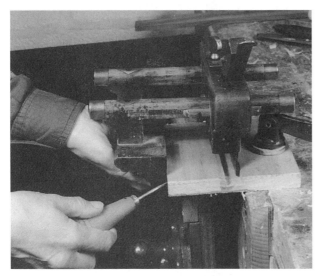

6-2 *Carefully set the distance between the edge of the board and the side of the groove, and then push the wedge keys home. Keeping in mind that the relationship between the fence and the workpiece decides the quality of the groove, make sure that the fence is held hard up to the left-hand edge of the board being worked.*

CUTTING THE THREE-REED MOLDING

6. When you have achieved the groove, then comes the good fun bit of using the reeding plane. Don't forget, it's all easy as long as you set the cutting iron for the finest cut and make sure that the sole of the plane is clean and waxed.

7. Set the plane rebate in the groove so that it is hard up against the left-hand side of the groove—and then to work. Take a series of cuts until the tops of the reeds are smooth and rounded.

8. Having cut the reeds on one side of the groove, turn the workpiece around so that you can work the other side, and rerun the procedure. Be mindful, all along the way, that the best cut is achieved if the rebated fence is held hard up against the side of the groove (*see* 6-3).

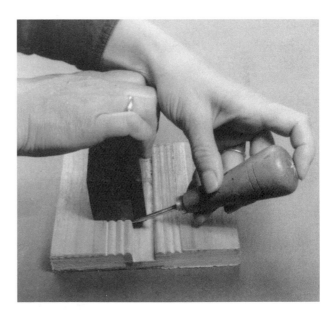

6-3 *Continue until the tops of the reeds are rounded and the left-hand side of the plane comes to rest on the surface of the wood.*

SPECIAL TIP

If and when you do decide to get yourself an old wooden reed molding plane, always check that the sole, the mouth, and the cutting iron are in good condition. The best-quality planes are the ones that have the reeded profiles made from inset strips of boxwood (*see* 6-4).

CUTTING THE ROUND NOSING

9. When you are happy with the groove and the reeding, take the 3/4-inch-thick 1 1/2-inch-wide strip that you have chosen for the drawer pull, and set it in the vise so that the grain direction runs away from you.

10. Take the hollow plane and set to work rounding the edge of the wood (*see* 6-5). There is almost nothing to say about this operation, other than to reiterate that it's as easy as falling off a log, but only as long as the iron is set for a whisker-thin cut and the sole is burnished with candle wax.

11. Finally, glue the pull strip in the groove, rub the whole works down to a smooth finish, burnish with beeswax . . . and the task is done.

6-4 Look for a plane that has a burnished box-wood sole and a clean, unbroken profile.

6-5 "Hollow" molding planes were made in a whole range of sizes. Broadly speaking, the width of any plane equals the radius of the part-circle curve of the sole.

AFTERTHOUGHTS

- Don't start out on this project by thinking that old wooden planes are going to cost you an arm and a leg—not a bit of it. We were able to purchase all three planes at a flea market/car boot sale for not much more than the cost of an average pair of shoes.
- Can this project be made with a power router? Yes, a power router is a great idea if you have plans to set up full-time production. But we strongly recommend using the old-fashioned molding planes since they are the perfect low-tech user-friendly tools for getting the job done—and they are very satisfying to work with. And keep in mind that the power router along with the three router bits will wind up costing you three or four times as much as the planes. And the whole router procedure is quite unpleasant—dusty, noisy, and altogether horrible!

SPECIAL TIP

When you are using wooden molding planes, much depends on the finished molded profile being uninterrupted and smooth. To this end, when the shape is complete, lightly run the plane backward and forward until the surface of the molding is burnished.

• Project 7 •

Laminated Knuckle Pin Hinge

Study the project pictures and the working drawings, and consider how the great thing about this project is the fact that it can be made from an easy-to-get, off-the-shelf section. All you need in fact is about 48 inches of a 3/8 x 3/8-inch-square section of wood and a 9-inch length of 1/8-inch-diameter dowel for each pair of hinges you want to make. That said, have a look at our step-by-step stages, and note how

the project focuses on making a pair of hinges. After all, who needs a single hinge?

As for your choice of wood, you can go for just about any type that takes your fancy—as long as it's reasonably straight grained and free from splits, knots, and the like.

Finally, look at the opposite page of inspirational drawings. Note how many alternatives may be built using the laminating technique.

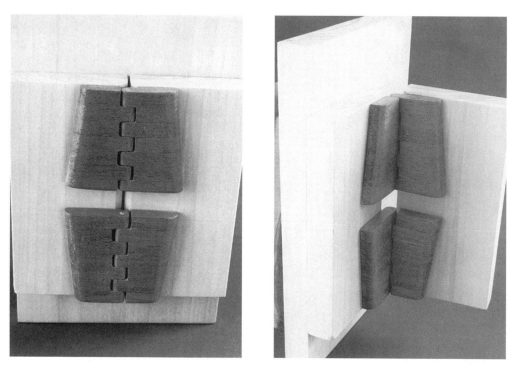

Project pictures—the finished project.

WOOD LIST

- A piece of furniture in the making that needs hinges—a door, box lid, swing hatch, screen, etc.
- A 48-inch length of 3/8 x 3/8-inch-square section of wood for each pair of hinges you want to make
- A 9-inch length of 1/8-inch-diameter dowel for each pairs of hinges—we use wooden barbecue skewers

SPECIAL TIP
Although our hinges are made from dark wood—sometimes mahogany—we wouldn't usually advocate using an endangered species. The wood was obtained as an off-cut that would otherwise have been burned.

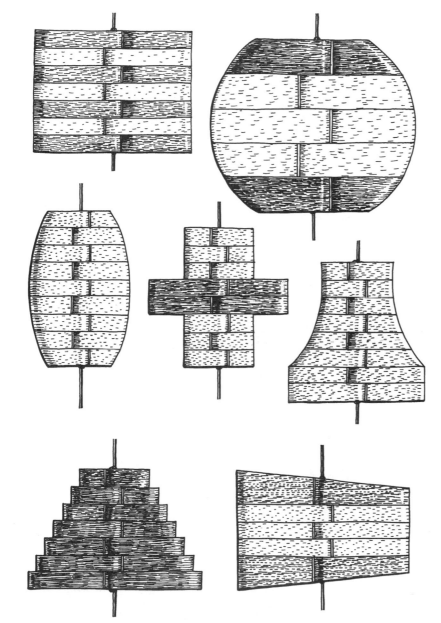

TOOLS & MATERIALS
- A small back saw—we use a gent's
- A good number of small clamps
- A pencil and ruler
- A drill with a 1/8-inch-diameter bit
- A small plane for rounding the knuckles
- A pair of dividers
- A good sharp knife for tidying up—we use a Swedish sloyd knife
- A sheet each of work-out and tracing paper
- All the usual workshop tools and materials . . . sandpaper, PVA glue, etc.

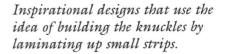

Inspirational designs that use the idea of building the knuckles by laminating up small strips.

CONSTRUCTION STAGES

Cutting & Arranging

1. Having studied our working drawings and the various stages, and seen how this project concentrates on building a pair of hinges, then have a final check to make sure that your wood is free from faults and go to work.

2. Take your chosen 3/8 x 3/8-inch-square section of wood—all planed and sanded—and use the pencil, ruler, and square to set it out in 3-inch lengths. To make the pair of hinges you need 14 lengths in all (see 7-1).

3. Keeping in mind that this project is about making two hinges at one and the same time, take the 3-inch lengths and arrange them side by side in two staggered stacks of seven (see 7-2). Make sure that every other line is staggered by 3/8 inch.

DRILLING, GLUING & CLAMPING

4. When you are happy with the arrangement, use a soft pencil to number the sequence—so that you know what goes where and how—and then use the dividers to set the ends out with center points and the 3/16-inch radius nosing. If you look at the working drawings below and the various step-by-step stages, you

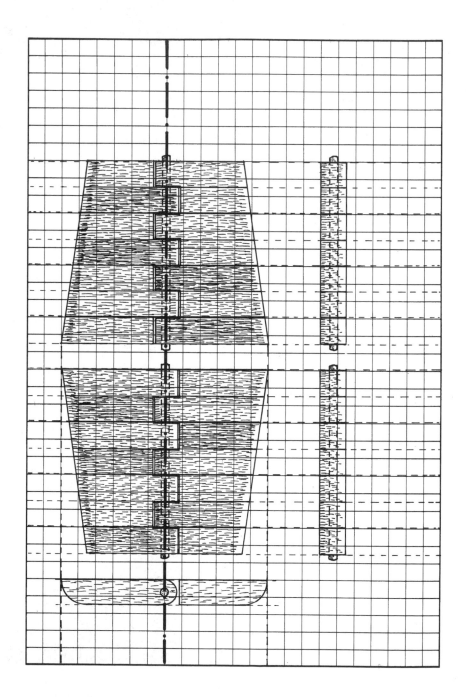

Working drawings—at a grid scale of four squares to an inch.

Note how the rounded knuckles have a radius of 3/16 inch, while the sides of the hinges are rounded over to a radius of 3/8 inch.

will see, in effect, that every single length has a nosing and a center point at one or other of its ends.

5. Make sure that the center points are well placed and then run them through with the 1/8-inch-diameter bit.

6. Reassemble the arrangement and have a dry-run fitting of the dowel pivots (*see* 7-3). You might have to trim back one or two of the ends in order to achieve a good fit.

7-1 Cut the 3/8 x 3/8-inch-square section into 3-inch lengths. It's important that the wood be well squared and finished, so spend time getting it right.

SPECIAL TIP

On finding that it is/was almost impossible to get small-sized doweling—meaning anything smaller than 1/4 inch—we started looking around for alternatives. We discovered that wooden cocktail sticks at a little larger than 1/16 inch diameter and wooden throwaway barbecue sticks at about 1/8 inch both do very nicely for projects that need these sizes.

7-2 If you play around with the strips, you will see that it is possible to achieve any number of hinge forms.

7-3 (Right) Trim the strips to a good length, tidy up the sawn ends and the holes, and then test the fit by running the three dowels in place.

7. Being very careful not to get glue on the drilled ends or near the dowel, smear glue on mating faces and clamp up (*see* 7-4).

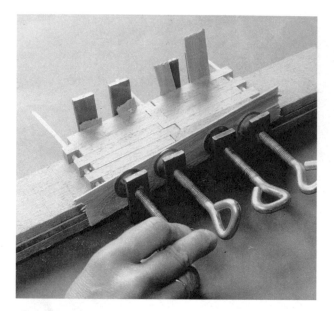

7-4 Use the smallest amount of glue to minimize the ooze-out, and have pieces of waste wood between the clamps and the workpiece.

CUTTING & FINISHING

8. When the glue is dry, take the pencil and ruler, and carefully set out the cutting lines. If you look closely at the working drawings and the drawing below (*see* 7-5), you will note how it is possible to achieve the pair of hinges by making two angled cuts.

9. Use a fine-toothed saw to cut the workpiece down into the four half-hinge pieces.

10. Now use the knife, plane, and sandpaper to round over the knuckle ends down to the 3/8-inch-diameter circle line. I found that the best way forward was to nip off the corners with the knife, then swiftly run the small plane over and around the ends, and then last of all tidy up with the sandpaper.

11. Link the halves with the dowel pivot and then continue with the fine-grade sandpaper until the hinge is a nicely rounded smooth-running fit.

12. Finally, round over the outer ends of the hinge—the angled edge (*see* 7-6)—give the whole works a good burnishing with wax polish, and the job is done.

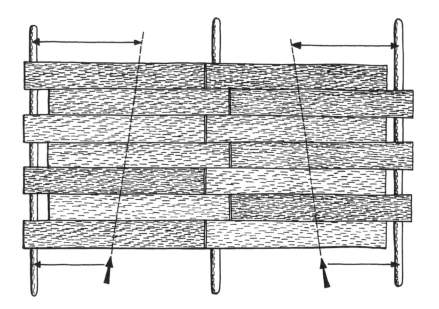

*7-5 Measure carefully from the dowel centers—
so that the half-hinges are identically tapered.*

AFTERTHOUGHTS

- We think that next time around we will rough out the rounded shape of the knuckles before gluing up.
- If you reckon to use off-cuts from your workshop stock—rather than buying in thin sections—then you could use a plane to run a nosing along one end-grain end of a board width and afterwards saw the wood down into little sticks before reassembling and gluing. This technique would ensure that the knuckles are all identical.
- If you want to go for a fancy hinge, then you could use two contrasting woods and alternate the colors when gluing up.

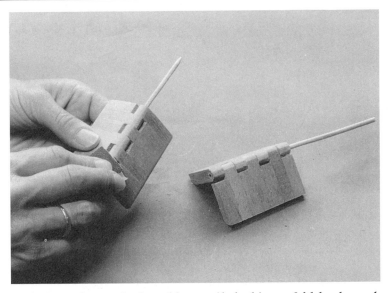

7-6 Round over the knuckles until the hinges fold backward and forward to a right angle.

• Project 8 •
Disk & Pin Hinge

This project draws its inspiration directly from a particular metal hinge that we observed on a piece of Chinese–European Art Deco style furniture. That is to say, the piece—a long low cupboard—was made in China in the 1920s to 1930s for the European market. Although the hinges were almost certainly designed in Europe to fit in with Art Deco imagery, by the time they had been worked on by Chinese craftsmen they seemed to us to have taken on a special "oriental" quality.

Have a look at the project pictures and the working drawings, and note how with this hinge there is an almost perfect coming together of design and function. Easy to make, perfect function, and a joy to the eyes—what more can you ask for?

As for your choice of wood, the design is such that, while it needs be unusually strong in thin sections, it also needs to be tight grained, free from splits and knots, and attractive in grain and color. This last point is particularly important, because the whole hinge is on show—it is an up-front part of the design. Nothing is hidden. Having considered a whole range of options, we went for our old favorite, English plum.

Project pictures—the finished project.

Have a look at the inspirational drawings below. Consider how there are one or two very interesting options on the two-plate-and-pin theme.

WOOD LIST

- A piece of furniture in the making that needs design feature hinges—a door, box lid, swing hatch, screen, or whatever

- Two pieces of 3/8-inch-thick wood at about 5 x 5 inches for each hinge that you want to make—this allows for a generous amount of cutting waste
- Two lengths of 1/4-inch-diameter dowel for each hinge

TOOLS & MATERIALS

- The use of a band saw
- A scroll saw—for the fine sawing
- A pencil and ruler
- A couple of 1/4-inch-wide U-section gouges—one shallow and one deep
- A pair of dividers
- A good sharp knife for tidying up—we use a Swedish sloyd knife
- A sheet each of work-out and tracing paper
- All the usual workshop tools and materials . . . sandpaper, PVA glue, etc.

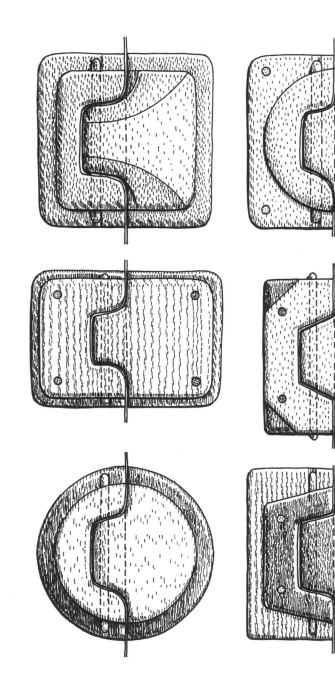

Inspirational designs that use the idea of two thicknesses and a channel to create a plate and pin hinge.

CONSTRUCTION STAGES

Setting Out & Cutting the Grooves

1. Our best advice with this project—before you do anything else—is to first have a look at the working drawings and observe how important it is that the pivot pin grooves be perfectly placed from one disk to the other.

2. Take the two pieces of carefully selected wood, pencil-label one side of each "back," and take that to mean the other side is the "best face." Try of course to have the most attractive side of the wood as the best face.

3. When you have a clear understanding of how the hinge works, take the dividers and scribe out two circles—the small one on the "back" face and at a radius of 1 1/2 inches, and the large one on the "best face" and at a radius of 2 inches.

4. With the grain running from top to bottom on both circles, take the pencil and ruler and set each circle out with four lines—one running through the center point, and three more lines being set at 1/4-inch step-offs to the side of the first diameter line (see 8-1). If you have it right, the centers of the circles are matched and all the lines are aligned.

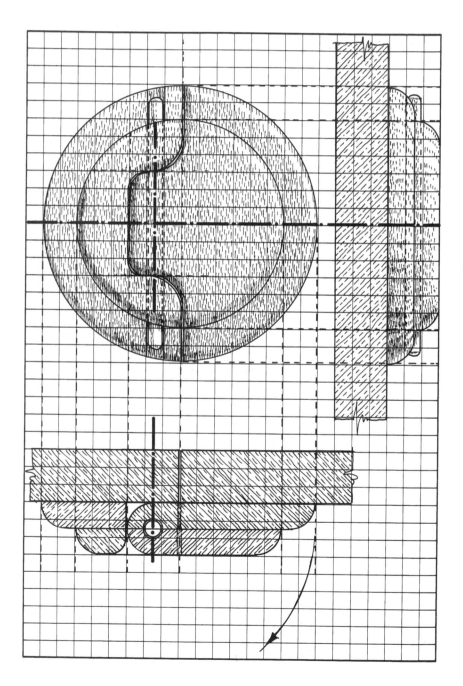

Working drawings—at a grid scale of four squares to an inch. Note how the two quarter-circle curves at the pivot add up to a total 3/4-inch-diameter half-circle knuckle.

5. Take the wood a piece at a time, butt it hard up against the bench hook, and use the two 1/4-inch-wide U-section gouges to scoop out the middle pivot channel. Aim for a neat scooped channel a shade over 1/4 inch wide and a tad over 1/8 inch deep (*see* 8-2).

CUTTING, FRETTING & FITTING.

6. Having scooped out the two channels—one on the best face of the large circle and the other on the back face of the small circle—move to the band saw and very carefully cut out the two disks (*see* 8-3). Go at it slowly so that any mistakes are made on the waste side of the drawn line.

8-1 (Top right) Use the utmost care and precision to set out the two circles with their accompanying lines.

8-2 (Middle right) Use a two-handed hold, one hand holding and guiding, and the other hand supplying the effort—the push.

8-3 (Bottom right) Our small band saw is fitted with a 1/4-inch blade, and is just narrow enough to run around a small disk of this size. We decided to use the band saw for cutting out the disk, rather than the scroll saw, because overall it makes for a swifter, easier cut.

7. With the two disks fretted out, take the pivot rod and have a trial fitting. If you have got it right, the pivot should be a loose, easy-slide fit, while at the same time you should be able to align the disks so that one is centered with the other (*see 8-4*).

8. When you have achieved a good fit, strap the two disks together with strips of sticky tape so that the binding is to the clear side of the centerline. Then meticulously draw out all the lines that go to make up the design.

9. Slide the pivot rod in place so that the two disks are held, aligned and locked, and then use the scroll saw to cut through the whole works. Of course you will ruin the length of dowel (for this project at least), but this procedure perfectly ensures that the two disks will stay put throughout (*see 8-5*).

SCULPTING & FINISHING

10. Having run a scroll saw cut through the whole sandwich—both disks and the dowel—remove all of the sticky tape, fit a new length of dowel in place in the channel, and then generally see how all of the component parts come together (*see 8-6*).

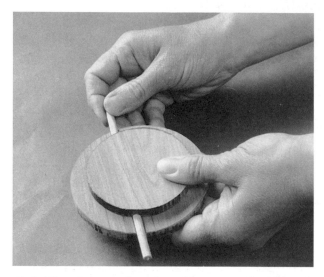

8-4 *The pivot needs to be a loose, easy fit. If need be, either adjust the channel and/or sand the dowel for a better fit.*

8-5 *Though leaving the dowel in place ruins it, this does ensure that the grooves are perfectly located.*

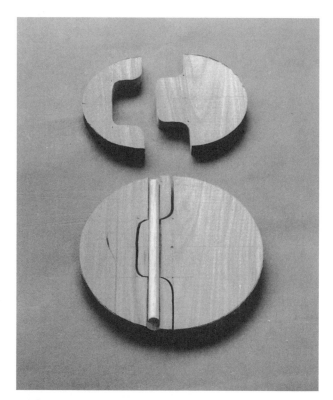

8-6 *This shot perfectly illustrates the need for a tight-grained strong hardwood, like plum. Loose-grained woods like pine and mahogany would almost certainly split down the length of the channel.*

8-7 Be careful when you are using the knife that you only carve in the direction of the grain—meaning from high to low wood. If you feel the blade beginning to run into the grain, turn the wood around and change the direction of the cut.

11. Before you go any further, stop a while and study the bottom center drawing of the working drawings. All that now remains is to round over the various sawn edges so that they all have quarter-circle curves with a radius of about 3/8 inch. Now see how the two quarter curves at either side of the pivot add up to a half-circle diameter of 3/4 inch.

12. Pencil-mark the edges that need to be curved—so that you don't make a mess-up and round over the wrong edge—then take the knife and swiftly go over the entire workpiece, slicing off the angles (*see* 8-7). Pay particular attention to the two part-circle curves that clasp the pivot at the center of the hinge.

13. With all the curves more or less whittled to shape with the knife, take the gouge and just as swiftly go over all the project to bring all the on-view surfaces to the same textured finish.

14. Smear glue on mating surfaces—and at the center part of the pivot dowel—and clamp the parts together. Last, wax, burnish or otherwise finish the hinge, glue and dowel the hinge in place on the piece of furniture—with the dowels on show or concealed—and the job is done.

AFTERTHOUGHTS

- This is one of those projects that can be made from off-cuts. I find that the best money-saving arrangement is to buy all my wood from the same supplier. What generally happens is that he is so keen to sell me the large, expensive lengths that he gives me all the small pieces free.

- If you want to go for a fancy design, then you could use two contrasting woods—say a light color for the small disk and the pivot pin, and a dark color for the large disk.

- Having said that you can use a knife and gouge to tidy up and to texture, it must also be said that these tools need to be razor sharp. My working procedure usually goes something like five minutes honing the tool, twenty minutes spent carving and whittling, five more minutes honing the tool, five minutes standing back and being critical, more carving and whittling, and so on. The rhythm of work—with tea and coffee breaks added—makes a pleasurable way of spending a day.

• Project 9 •

Inset Screen Hinge

There are two difficulties in making wooden hinges for a screen that needs to be zigzagged like a concertina. The first is: how to design a hinge that folds in both directions. The second problem is: how to fit such a hinge when you can't get access to drill holes. If you have a good long look at the project pictures and the working drawings, you will see how this project very nicely solves these problems—with the integral hinge folding in any direction and back on itself, and with the planed groove with the inset strip doing away with the need for drilling holes in the body of the screen.

As for your choice of wood, you can just about go for any type that takes your fancy. We have used tulip poplar for the body of the screen, American cherry for the hinge blocks, and straight-grained cedar for the strips.

Have a look at the inspirational drawings on the opposite page and consider that there are a great many possibilities based on the strip and block theme.

Project pictures—the finished project.

WOOD LIST

- A screen in the making that needs integral wooden hinges
- Lengths of 1/4-inch-thick strip wood for the inset—to suit the size and design of your screen
- A 3-inch length of 3/4-inch-thick wood at 1 1/2 inches wide for each hinge
- A quantity of 1/4-inch-diameter dowel to suit your screen

TOOLS & MATERIALS

- A plow plane for cutting the grooves—we use a Stanley 45
- A wooden "hollow" plane at 3/8 inch wide—for working the round nosing
- A band saw or scroll saw
- A pencil and ruler
- A drill press with a 1/4-inch-diameter Forstner bit
- A two-pin marking gauge
  - A pair of dividers
  - A good sharp knife for tidying up—we use a Swedish sloyd knife
  - A sheet each of work-out and tracing paper
  - All the usual workshop tools and materials . . . sandpaper, PVA glue, etc.

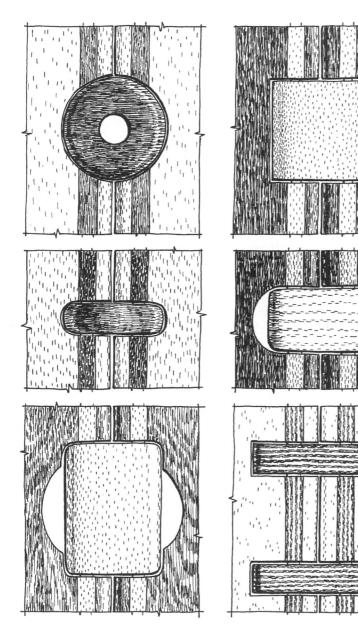

Inspirational designs that use the idea of grooves and blocks to make a screen hinge.

CONSTRUCTION STAGES

Setting Out & Cutting the Grooves

1. When you have studied this project, to the extent that you are absolutely clear as to how the project needs to be made and put together, take your chosen wood—meaning the wood that you are using for the side frame or stiles of the screen—and pencil-mark the edges that need to be hinged.

2. Now take your marking knife, or your two-pin marking gauge, and run two scribed lines down the side face of the workpiece to mark the position of the groove.

NOTE
While we decided to run the two grooves—one on either side of a centerline, and then saw down the center so as to make two matched frame members—you might well decide to work individual members. Either way, the 1/4-inch-wide channel needs to be set 1/4 inch in from the screen edge.

3. Fit your chosen plow plane up with a 1/4-inch-wide blade, set the depth gauge foot to a depth of 1/2 inch, and set the fence to suit your method of working.

4. With the guidelines in place, and with the workpiece held secure so that the side fence of the plane runs clear of the bench, take the plane and make the first cut. It's all easy enough, as

Working drawings—at a grid scale of four squares to an inch. Note especially the total 3/4-inch-diameter half-circle profile of the block knuckle—shown in cross section at the bottom.

long as you make sure that the plane is held upright and the fence is pressing hard up against the edge of the workpiece.

5. And so you continue, making repeated passes until the 1/4-inch-wide channels are cut to a depth of 1/2 inch (*see* 9-1).

6. With the groove crisply worked, then have a dry fit with the dowel. If all is well, the dowel should sit in the groove centered within the 3/4-inch-thickness of the wood (*see* 9-2).

SPECIAL TIP

Although we generally advise beginners that using a plow plane is a wonderfully enjoyable activity—and it is truly great fun to see the ribbons of waste curl up from the plane—we always add a proviso: Only use it if the cutter is razor sharp and set to take the thinnest of thin cuts, and if the sole and fence are burnished with candle wax.

Then again, if the cutter is dull and set to cut at too great a depth, it all adds up to a miserable muscle-aching experience.

9-1 *The difficulty when using a combination plane to work a relatively narrow section is how to secure the wood without obstructing the run. Note how this is overcome by having the fence hanging over the edge of the bench, and the rods on the right-hand side of the plane just clearing the holdfast.*

FRETTING & DRILLING

7. When you are satisfied that all is correct, take your matched edges—both with grooves—and use a pencil, ruler, and square to draw out the locating notches or step-backs. The total step-back needs to be 3 inches long and 1 1/2 inches deep—that is, 3/4 inches into each side.

9-2 *The grooves need to be 1/2 inch deep—so that there is 1/4-inch headroom when the 1/4-inch dowels are in place.*

9-3 *Though we used a band saw to clear the waste, you could just as well use a hand coping saw.*

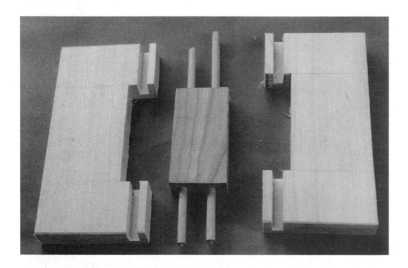

8. Use the band saw to cut out the step-backs. The best procedure is to first make two straight cuts to establish the depth, and then clean out the waste with two secondary cuts (*see* 9-3).

9. Cut the 3 x 1 1/2-inch-block to fit and drill 1/4-inch holes in the end of the block to line up with the grooves. Pop lengths of dowel in the grooves and have a trial fit (*see* 9-4).

FINISHING & FITTING

10. When you have achieved a good fit of the block-and-dowel component in the grooves, then remove the dowels and start working the sides of the block and the sides of the grooved boards. Plane down to a half-circle nosing (*see* 9-5). You should be aiming for a 3/4-inch-diameter half-circle profile with the dowels and holes at the center.

9-4 *(Left) The dowel-block component should slot neatly into place—with the dowel stubs sitting in the grooves.*

9-5 *If you can't get to use a wooden "hollow" plane, then you could shape the curves with a knife and block plane.*

11. Slide the dowel in the block, fit the whole works in place, and then set the 3/8-inch strips in the grooves (*see* 9-6).

12. Finally, having first tested that the three component parts slide over each other (*see* 9-7), glue the strips in place and plane down to a good finish. Use a small block plane.

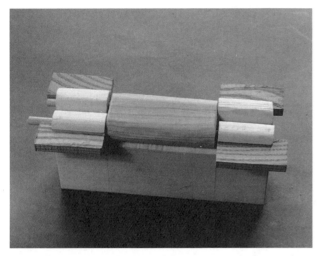

9-6 Use the graded sandpapers to rub down the curves to the extent that the two flaps are able to fold back and touch—so that they smoothly roll over each other.

9-7 (Right) When you reach a point where the curves roll over each other, then is the time to glue the strips in place for the final planing and rubbing down.

AFTERTHOUGHTS

• Keeping in mind that the grooves get to be cut two-thirds of the way into the 3/4-inch thickness, you do have to be careful not to split the wood.

• If you can't get to use a plow plane, then you could just about cut the grooves with a scoring knife and 1/4-inch-wide chisel.

• We had some difficulties with the plow plane—simply because we were working with a short length of wood. The good news is: The longer the wood, the easier it is!

• For added strength, you could have the grain running across the hinge block.

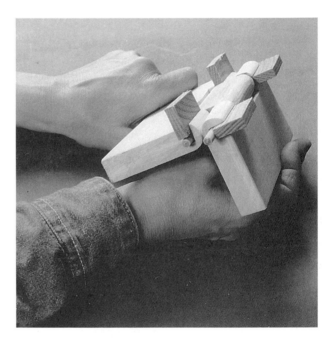

• Project 10 •
Rule Hinge

There I was, sitting at my bench and wondering how to come up with a design for an integral hinge that could be fitted to the edge of a pair of doors or a screen—so that the doors/screens could be folded back on themselves—when, right in front of me, the hinge on my boxwood and brass rule caught my eye (*see* 10-1). If you look at the project pictures below and the working drawings, you will see that this hinge—copied more or less directly from the ruler—makes for a very neat solution. The design is

such that the hinge can be put together from a number of easy-to-make components.

As for the choice of wood, the primary need is for a wood that is tight grained, attractive in character, and strong. Once again we decided to go for American cherry for the door, English plum for the hinge plates, and a shop-bought dowel for the pivot rod.

Have a look at the inspirational drawings on the opposite page for insight into some of the possible ideas you might use.

Project pictures—the finished project.

WOOD LIST
- A piece of furniture in the making that needs integral edge hinges—with solid 3/4-inch-thick doors
- A quantity of 3/8-inch-thick wood—to suit the size and design of your piece of furniture
- A quantity of 1/4-inch-diameter dowel to suit

TOOLS & MATERIALS
- A scroll saw
- A pencil and ruler
- A bullnose plane
- A chisel for paring
- A drill press with Forstner bits at 1/16 and 1/4 inch diameter
- A pair of dividers
- A good sharp knife for tidying up—we use a Swedish sloyd knife
- A sheet each of work-out and tracing paper
- All the usual workshop tools and materials . . . sandpaper, PVA glue, etc.

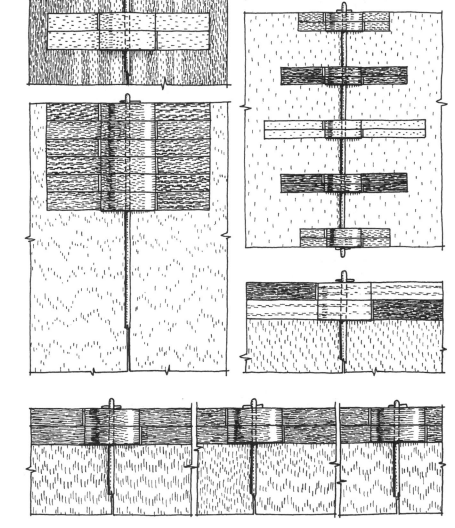

Inspirational designs that use ruler-type hinges in the design.

CONSTRUCTION STAGES

Setting Out & Fretting the Hinge Plates

1. When you have collected your tools and considered how the hinges need to be modified to suit your piece of furniture, then have another look at the working drawings and see how you need eight profiles for each pair of hinges that you want to make. You need: four with-circle strips, and four strips with the circles cut away.

2. Start by cutting your wood down into 1 1/2-inch-wide strips and planing it so that one edge is true.

3. Take a strip slightly longer to suit your piece of furniture, set out the 1 1/2-inch width with a line 3/4 inch in from the true edge, establish a center and pivot point, and then use the dividers to set out a circle with a radius of 1/2 inch (*see* the working drawings, bottom middle).

4. With all the lines of the design in place, take all your strips and pin them together in stacks so that the design strip is uppermost. We decid-ed to go for two stacks of three—so that we would have a few spares in case of mess-ups.

5. Not forgetting that both sides of the hinge share a common cutting line, move to the scroll saw and very carefully fret out the design. If you are doing it right, each 1 1/2-inch-wide strip will give you two component parts and a long length of waste (*see* 10-2).

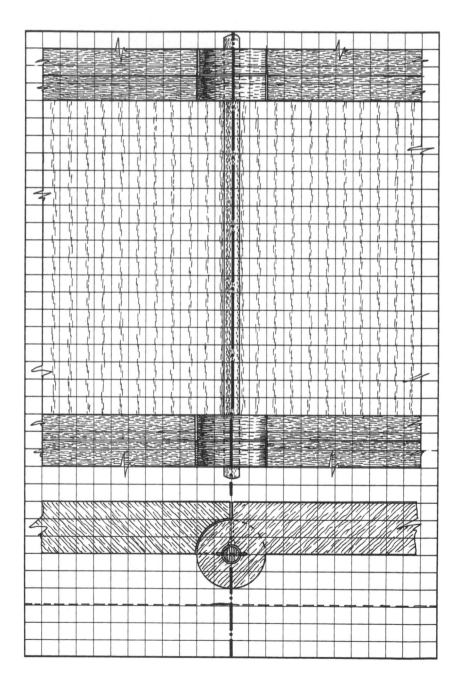

Working drawings—at a grid scale of four squares to an inch.
Study the section at middle bottom, and see how the edge of the doors, or the door and stile—the two edges that meet at the hinge—need to be chamfered to allow room for the pivot to run from one hinge to the other.

PUTTING TOGETHER

6. When you have achieved the eight parts—four with circle strips and four strips without—run 1/4-inch-diameter holes through the pivot points and then pair the parts up so that you have four identical components (see 10-3). This done, make sure that the true back edges and the circles are perfectly aligned, and then glue them together.

7. Take the four identical components and pivot them, turn and turn about, on a length of dowel until you have what you consider are the best two hinges (see 10-4). If one or other of the parts needs easing, then use a knife and sandpaper to cut the edges back for a good fit.

SPECIAL TIP

Don't forget that while our project shows how the hinges might be used to link, say, two folds of a screen, or maybe a box to its lid, you might well use the hinges to link a door to its stile or whatever. This being so, be mindful that you might well have to modify the fitting accordingly.

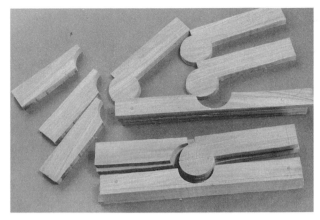

10-2 It's just as well that we decided to cut a few spares, because two of the cutouts came to grief when they split across the grain.

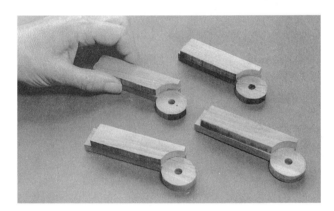

10-3 Don't be fooled into making mirror-image opposites—you need four identical components.

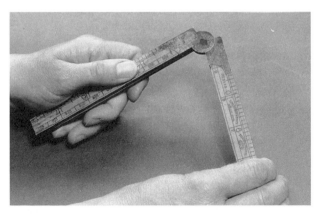

10-1 The important thing to note with the ruler hinge is the way the pivot point occurs, in effect, at the corners of the ruler.

10-4 Fiddle, fuss, and trim the components so that you have two complete hinges. Be very careful not to force the action—it needs to be smooth and easy.

10-5 Be very watchful when you are clamping up that you don't crush and do damage to the wood. In this instance you only need a small amount of pressure—just enough to force out a thin bead of glue.

8. When you have sorted out what goes where and how, trim the mating faces to a flush fit—that is, the edges of the door and the faces of the hinges—chamfer the sides of the door that meet at the pivot, and then glue, pin, and clamp the hinges in place (*see* 10-5). Make sure that the back of the hinges and the back of the door are flush.

FINISHING

9. Take the door with the hinges fitted, set it faceup with the hinges farthest away from you, and butt it hard up against a bench stop. This done, use the bullnose plane and the chisel to skim the hinge flush with the face of the door (*see* 10-6 and 10-7). Aim for a clean-cut angle where the circle part of the hinge meets the door.

10-6 (Left) Although the low angle blade of this little Record plane makes it a good tool for small skimming cuts, the bullnose design leaves a small amount of waste that has to be pared back with a chisel.

10-7 Be sure when you are paring back with the chisel that you are ready to brake if you feel the tool running out of control.

● *Project 13—Recessed Folk Art Flower Knob*

● *Project 2—Pierced & Sculpted Hole Handle*

● *Project 3—Pierced Arts & Crafts Handle*

A

● *Project 8—Disk & Pin Hinge*

● *Project 10—Rule Hinge*

● *Project 12—Stickley Arts & Crafts Knob*

● Project 15—Turned Mushroom Knob

● Project 1—Laminated
Bridge Handle

● Project 7—Laminated Knuckle Pin Hinge

● Project 18—Turned &
Recessed Knob

● *Project 23—Leaf Spring Latch*

● *Project 11—Inset Dovetail Hinge Plate*

H

10. And so you continue, sanding the face of the door to a smooth finish, rounding over the side edges (*see* 10-8), rubbing the edges of the hinge down to a slightly rounded finish, and so on, until you have two well-matched component parts (*see* 10-9).

10-8 Rough out the curved edge with the plane and then use the sandpaper to rub the workpiece down to a smooth finish.

10-9 At this stage of the game, you should have two more or less identical component parts.

11. Finally, slot the hinges together, link and pivot both hinges with a single dowel that runs right across the door, drill and peg the dowel ends so that everything stays put (*see* 10-10), and the job is done.

AFTERTHOUGHTS

- You must always remember, when you read through the various stages, that you will almost certainly have to modify the project to suit your door, screen, piece of furniture, or whatever.
- If you do decide to cut parts out in stacked multiples—as shown in this project—then you must make sure that the blade is new and well tensioned. We say this because, if the blade is dull and slack, then chances are it will curve and sag—in which case the line of cut will wander through the stack and you will be left with ill-matched cutouts.

10-10 If you had in mind to use this hinge on a screen, then you could cut the dowel ends flush and have the pins on the door side of the hinge.

• Project 11 •
Inset Dovetail Hinge-Plate

Although with most of the projects our little stand with its door or doors is no more than an easy means of displaying the hinge, catch, or whatever, in this project the two little doors in which the hinge is set are in fact part and parcel of the hinge. We say this because although you could cut the dovetail shape in, say, the two side edges of a screen, you wouldn't be able to drill into the end grain of the main body to fit the pivots. The drill bit wouldn't be long enough. This is without doubt one of the most attractive and easy-to-make projects in the book.

If you study the project pictures and the working drawings, you will note that the hinge is made up of three component parts: the two sides with the cutout areas and the central dovetail inset that links the two.

As for wood, we decided to use tulip polar for the two flaps, and a small piece of found driftwood for the dovetail inset—it seems to be old mahogany.

Take a look at the inspirational drawings on the opposite page that explore and explain the theme of inset dovetail hinges.

Project pictures—the finished project.

WOOD LIST

- A piece of 3/4-inch-thick wood at about 5 inches wide and 6 inches long for each hinge that you want to make
- A piece of 1-inch-thick wood 2 1/4 inches long and 1 3/4 inches wide for each dovetail inset
- A couple of short lengths of 1/4-inch-diameter dowel

TOOLS & MATERIALS

- A scroll saw, or a band saw with a thin blade
- A pencil and ruler
- A drill press with Forstner bit at 1/4-inch diameter
- A pair of dividers
- A good sharp knife for tidying up—we use a Swedish sloyd knife
- A sheet each of work-out and tracing paper
  - All the usual workshop tools and materials . . . sandpaper, PVA glue, etc.

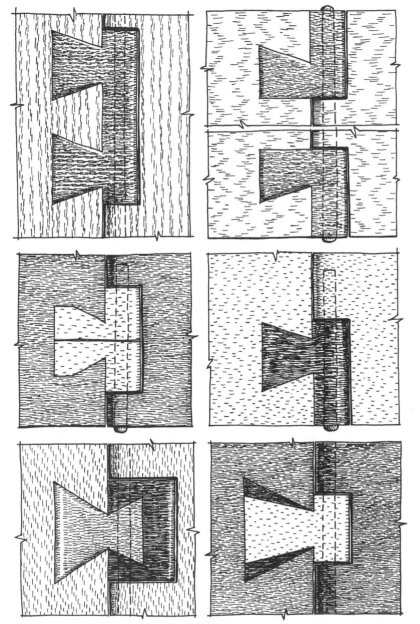

Inspirational designs that use the idea of dovetails and insets.

CONSTRUCTION STAGES

Setting Out, Fretting & Fitting

1. When you have collected your tools, chosen your wood, and generally got yourself ready to work, take the 5 x 6-inch piece of wood, decide on the best face, and then set it out with a centerline that runs in the direction of the grain.

2. Having first studied the working drawings, use the pencil ruler and square to set out the shape of the dovetail inset (*see* 11-1).

3. Run the centerline through on the band saw and then cut out the two sides of the inset (*see* 11-2). Aim all along the way to steer the line of cut slightly to the waste side of the drawn line.

SPECIAL TIP
If you compare the working drawings and the finished project with the early photographs, you may well notice that at some stage we decided to reduce the width of the plain side of the inset by 1/4 inch. This doesn't affect the workings of the project, and I can't remember now why I did it. The point I am making is that it's OK to change the design to suit your needs—as long as the changes don't make a mess of the working action.

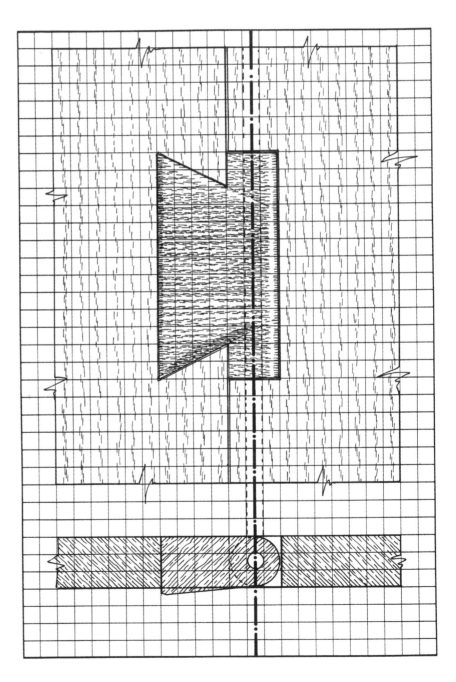

Working drawings—at a grid scale of four squares to an inch. Note how in the section at middle bottom, the dovetail part of the inset is slightly sculpted so that it stands proud of its surround.

4. Set the two halves down on the piece of inset wood so that the two sides are touching along the centerline. Then use a knife to scribe exactly around the inside edge of the inset hole. Be careful to make sure that the scribed line remains true.

5. Take the wood with the scribed profile and cut it out on the band saw. Once again, go at it nice and slowly, all the while making sure that the line of cut is to the waste side of the scribed line. If you have done it correctly, the inset will be a tight push-fit (*see* 11-3).

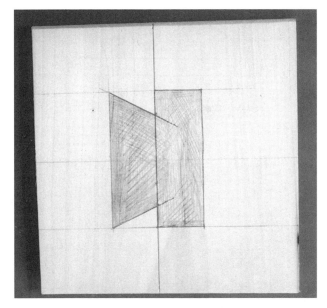

11-1 Draw out the shape of the dovetail inset so that it is aligned on the centerline.

11-3 If you have made a good cut, then the parts will be a tight push-fit and lock together.

11-2 The best procedure for clearing the waste with the band saw is to first run two cuts to establish the depth, then make a long, slow, curved cut to one or other of the depth cuts, and then to clear the remaining waste with a final cut.

DRILLING, SANDING & PUTTING TOGETHER

6. Smear a small amount of glue on the dovetail—the inset and the mortise—and gently tap the two together. Wipe away excess glue.

7. Having waited for the glue to set, and trued up the edges of the 5 x 6-inch workpiece with the block plane, then use the pencil, ruler, and dividers to fix the position of the pivot points and to draw out the 3/4-inch-diameter knuckles (refer to the bottom center of the working drawings).

8. With a long-shanked 1/4-inch-diameter Forstner bit fitted in the pillar drill, set the workpiece together and support it on the drill table so that it is perfectly upright. Use clamps or blocks to steady the arrangement and then run a 1/4-inch-diameter hole down into the edge of the outer block and on down into the inset (*see* 11-4). It's particularly important that the holes are well aligned—so take the time you need to get it right.

9. When you are happy with the position of the holes, take the knife and sandpaper, and set to work rounding over the nosings or knuckles. All you do is use the knife to slice away the bulk of the rough and then tidy up with the block and sandpaper. Aim for a crisp half-circle that rolls over so that the main part of the dovetail is left standing slightly proud (*see* 11-5).

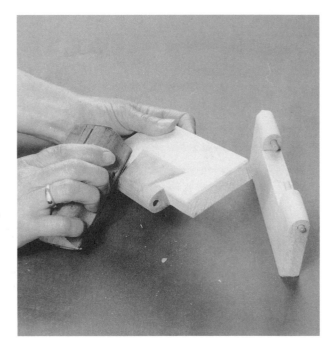

11-5 (Above) Round over the knuckles so that the dovetail part of the inset is left standing slightly proud, and then use a scrap of sandpaper to sculpt the edges of the dovetail.

11-4 (Left) It's important that the holes be right the first time around, so if you are a beginner, or if you have any doubts, then have several tryouts on scrap wood.

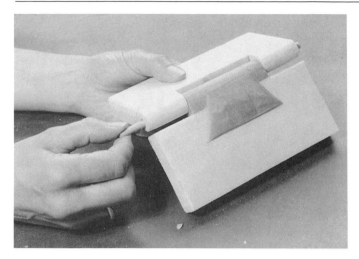

11-6 If you look at this photograph, you will see how the inset could be fitted in a chest—the dovetail part of the inset in the lid and the rounded part fitted at the top of the back edge. The only thing you would have to figure out is how to drill a hole in from one edge to run through the knuckle of the inset and beyond.

10.   And so you continue, whittling, scraping, and sanding, until both halves of the hinge roll over each other with a nice, smooth movement (*see* 11-6).

11.   Finally, glue the dowel pivots in place, and sand all the surfaces to a smooth finish. Now the hinge is ready for attaching to your cupboard, box, door, etc.

AFTERTHOUGHTS

• If you can figure out how to drill the hole, then this hinge would look good inset directly into the body of a box lid.

• Having pondered about how to drill deep holes, I see that this could be done relatively easily with a hand auger bit. For example, I have an old fluted auger that will drill a hole about 18 inches deep. Certainly it might take a bit of practice—but it could be done.

• Project 12 •
Stickley Arts & Crafts Knob

If you are interested in plain oak furniture, and if you enjoy simple, direct, honest forms of construction, then you can't do better than search out the work of the great American Arts & Crafts furniture maker Gustav Stickley (1857–1942). His work is characterized by the use of plain oak, lots of bold square sections, through-tenons, and by carefully worked details.

This project draws its inspiration from a Stickley wooden drawer pull, as used on his now famous Mission furniture. This knob is charac-terized by being square and faceted with a pyramidal end profile. Have a look at the project pictures and the working drawings.

This is surely one of the easiest projects in the book. OK, so oak is a bit difficult to sand, but then again, the basic knob can be cut out in just a few minutes. That said, a good part of the success of this knob—its strength and quality of design—has to do with the fact that the square section stem, or tenon, has to be let into a square mortise. Or to put it another way, if you

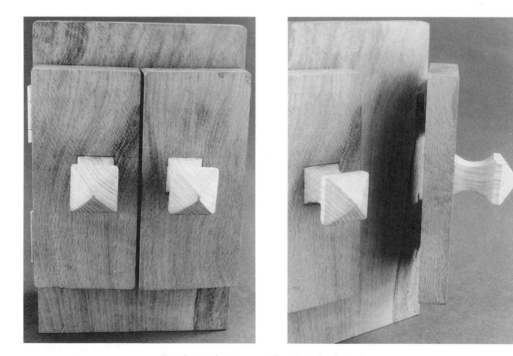

Project pictures—the finished project.

enjoy cutting mortises, then this project is going to be fun. On the other hand, if you hate cutting mortises, then have a look at the inspirational designs below and note how any number of basic knob forms can be achieved by the simple technique of fretting a square section.

As regards the choice of wood, I think that the strength of the design has to do with the fact that the knob is made of oak. No messing, no exotic woods—just oak.

WOOD LIST

- A length of 1 3/16 x 1 3/16-inch square section of American oak—a 3-inch length for each knob that you want to make

TOOLS & MATERIALS

- An electric fret saw—we use a Hegner
- A drill press with a Forstner drill bit at about 3/4-inch diameter
- A 3/4-inch straight chisel—either chamfer edged or a mortise
- A roll of double-sided sticky tape
- A pencil, ruler, and set square
- A small width, shallow-sweep straight gouge
- A good sharp knife—we use a Swedish sloyd knife
- A sharpening stone
- A bench fitted with a vise
- A bench holdfast
- A sheet each of work-out and tracing paper
- A pack of graded sandpapers—and wet or dry papers

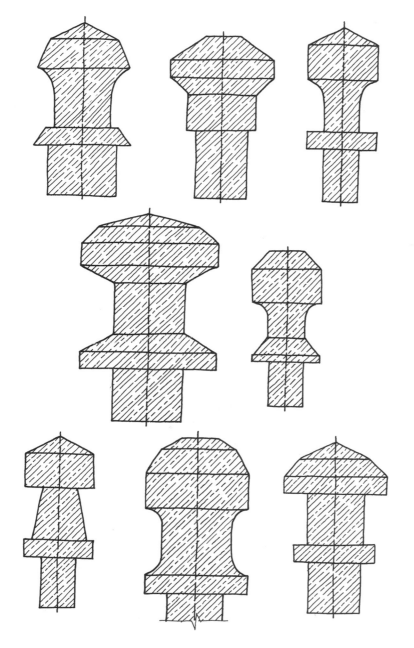

Inspirational designs—eight designs based on simple faceted forms.

CONSTRUCTION STAGES

Setting Out the Design & Fretting

1. When you have chosen your piece of wood, have set out your tools so that they are close at hand, and have generally prepared yourself for the task ahead, draw the design up to full size and make a clear tracing.

2. Having first used the square to set the wood out with guidelines that correspond with the primary lines of the design, carefully align the tracing on one or other of the faces of the wood and press-transfer the traced lines. Do this on two neighboring faces. Shade in all the areas of waste so that there will not be any misunderstanding about which pieces need to be cut away (*see* 12-1).

3. When you are happy with the way the design has been set out, move to the scroll saw and cut out the profile as seen in one view. Aim for a minimum of cuts—so that the waste comes away as three pieces (*see* 12-2).

4. Stick double-sided tape on the sawn faces and press the waste pieces back in place so as to remake the square-faced block.

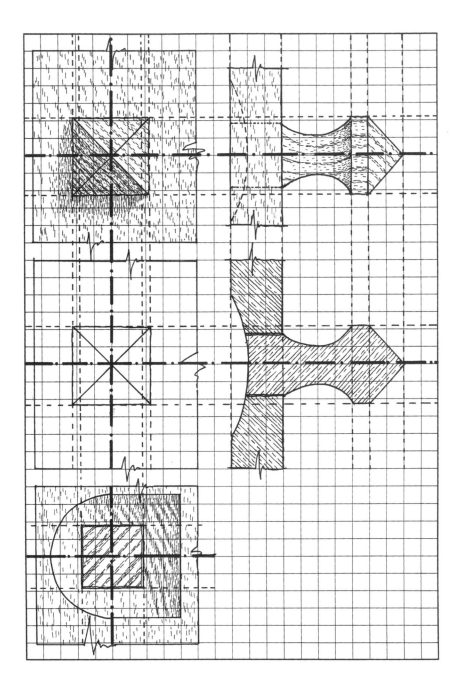

Working drawings—at a grid scale of four squares to an inch.

Note especially the cross-section detail at bottom right that shows how the wood is scooped out at the back of the knob.

5. Finally repeat the sawing procedure as already described, only this time cut the profile out as seen in the other view (*see* 12-3).

SANDING

6. By the time you have run the workpiece through the scroll saw—first for one face and then for the other—the knob should be more or less finished.

7. Start by sanding the pyramid end. All you do is wrap the sandpaper around a flat batten—so that the sanding side is uppermost—and then move the workpiece backward and forward. Work the facets, turn and turn about—always in the direction of the grain—until the four faces are crisp and well centered (*see* 12-4).

12-3 Although the sawing is pretty easy, you do have to watch out that the top slice of waste doesn't catch and buck up.

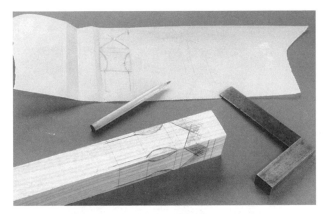

12-1 Spend time making certain that the design is crisply and clearly set out on the wood.

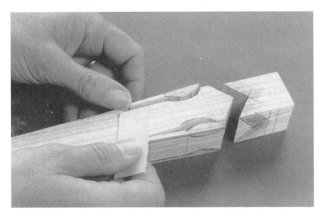

12-2 Use double-sided sticky tape to fit the slices of waste back in place.

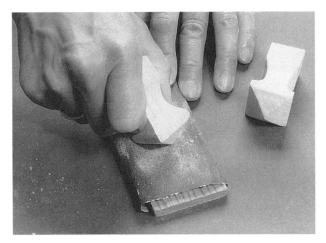

12-4 Be careful, when you are sanding, that you don't round over and blur the angles.

8. When you come to the curved neck, all you do is wrap the sandpaper around a piece of 1/2-inch-diameter dowel—so as to make a sanding stick—and then use the stick in much the same way as you would a file or rasp. Once again, rub the curved sides down, turn and turn about, until you have achieved sides and angles that are clean and crisp (*see* 12-5).

MORTISING & FINISHING

9. Now for the not-so-easy task of cutting the mortise and fitting. Make decisions as to where you want the knob to be attached and then use the ruler and square to set out the guidelines accordingly. Align the knob with the guidelines and use a knife or hard pencil to draw around the tenon.

10. When you are happy that everything is just so, move to the drill press and run the 3/4-inch-diameter hole through the center of the drawn square.

11. Position the workpiece flat down on the bench, secure it with the holdfast (*see* 12-6), and then set to work cutting the mortise. It's beautifully easy; all you do is slice back little by little from the hole until you reach the drawn line (*see* 12-7). When you have achieved a tight push-fit, smear PVA glue on the inside face of the mortise and tap the knob home.

SPECIAL TIP

If, like us, you make a bit of a mess of the back of the mortise—maybe with gaps and a bit of grain damage—then now is the time to make good. It's a very easy procedure; all you do is dip little slivers of off-cut in glue and tap then into the gaps.

12-5 Sand around and around the neck so as to leave the widest part of the knob looking crisp and square.

12-6 (Right) Pencil-label the knob tenon so that you know precisely how it relates to the mortise.

12-8 Run the gouge from the side through to center.

12-7 (Left) Hold the chisel upright and work with a tightly controlled paring stroke. Be very careful that you don't force the pace and so split the wood.

12. Last, turn the workpiece over so that the back of the drawer or door is uppermost, and then use the gouge to scoop out a depression that centers on the knob. Aim for a nice simple scooped form like a circle or part-circle (*see* 12-8). Keep in mind that the function of the depression—the scooped area—is twofold; it adds a certain amount of decorative interest, and the dappled texture of the carving helps to disguise small mess-ups.

AFTERTHOUGHTS
- The sanding is hard work. But you can minimize this by making a really good job of the sawing.
- The main function of the scooped depression at the back of the handle was to hide our badly cut mortise. We do think that the shape and texture of the dappled carving does make a pleasant contrast to the rather smooth and severe lines of the knob.

• Project 13 •
Recessed Folk Art Flower Knob

There was in pre-twentieth-century Europe a wonderful lively folk art tradition of cutting and carving knobs and furniture pulls in the form of natural objects. There are Polish and Czech knobs that are of birds and snails, Swiss and German knobs of little human faces, Swedish knobs in the form of mushrooms, flowers, and buds, and so on.

I don't know too much about all the whens and whys, other than to say that this tradition must surely have had its beginnings in the simple desire by working folk to copy what they saw in nature. So, for example, when they wanted to make a little knob for a drawer or maybe a box, it was the most natural thing in the world to draw inspiration from their workaday experiences in the fields and woods. They wouldn't have known anything about design, or big-city fashion; they just copied nature.

Have a look at the project pictures below and the working drawings and consider how this project draws its inspiration directly from a little flower form—nothing fancy, just a delightful archetypal daisy-type flower set in a shallow scooped recess. If you like whittling and carving, then you are going to really enjoy this project.

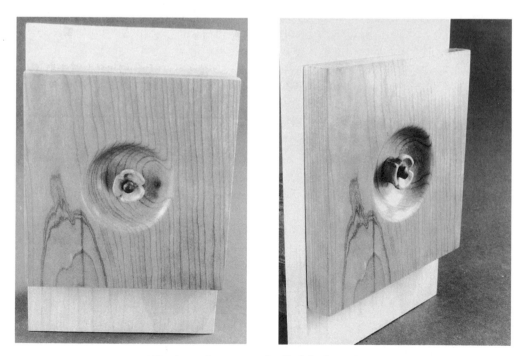

Project pictures—the finished project.

There are many design possibilities that derive from the simple idea of carving a knob that looks like a natural plant form.

As to the choice of wood, the relatively small size and delicacy of the flower—the outer petal shape and the small peg at the center—dictate that the wood be tight grained and strong. Traditional woods like lime, beech, pine, sycamore, box, cherry, and maple are fine. We chose to use European boxwood for the flower, a scrap of English plum for the knob at the center of the flower, and American cherry for the recessed base board—that is, the drawer/cupboard front.

WOOD LIST

- A length of 1 x 1-inch-square section of boxwood—a 2-inch-length for each flower that you want to carve
- A scrap of wood for the central knob—to contrast with the color of the petals

TOOLS & MATERIALS

- A small low-angled plane for roughing out—we use an old Record bullnose rabbet plane No. 076
- A pencil, ruler, and a pair of dividers
- Good sharp knives for whittling—we use a Swedish sloyd knife and an old penknife
- A small straight gouge for scooping out the recess
- A bench hook
- A bench drill press
- Forstner bits in the sizes 5/8 inch and 1/8 inch
- A sheet each of work-out and tracing paper
- All the usual workshop tools and materials . . . sandpaper, PVA glue, dividers, scissors, etc.

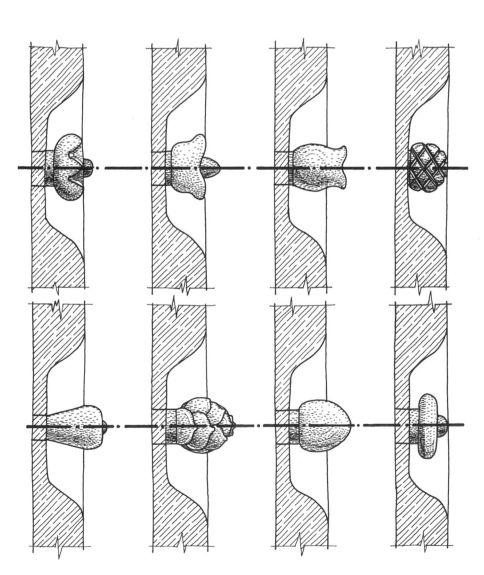

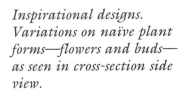

Inspirational designs. Variations on naïve plant forms—flowers and buds—as seen in cross-section side view.

CONSTRUCTION STAGES

Setting Out the Design

1. When you have selected your wood, and honed your knives to a razor-sharp edge, take your chosen length of wood and check it over for possible flaws. It's most important that the grain be straight and free from splits and knots.

2. Study the working drawings to the extent that you have a clear understanding of the order of work.

Then take your pencil, ruler, and compass, and set out all the lines that go to make up the design. Have the circle on your item of furniture—the circle for the scooped area or recessed area—at a diameter of 3 inches and the circle for the flower at 1 inch. Use the 1/2-inch compass radius to set the end of the flower out with the six-point motif (*see* 13-1).

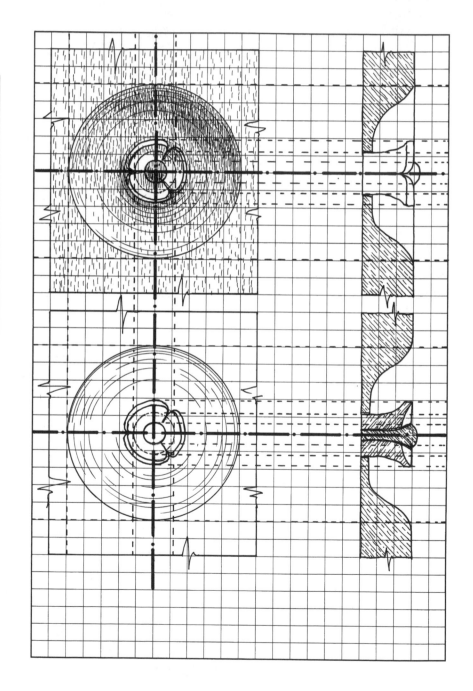

> **SPECIAL TIP**
> Whoever it was that first said "a sharp knife is safer than a blunt one" must certainly have been a whittler. If you find that you have to force and bully your knife through the wood, then you can be pretty certain that it is blunt, you are wasting effort, and that the whole procedure is dangerous. Your knives must literally be as sharp as a razor. Try to develop a rhythm of working something like: (1) a few minutes spent whittling, (2) a minute or so standing back from the work to look at it with a critical eye, (3) a minute or so honing the blade, (4) then back to whittling, and so on.

Working drawings—at a grid scale of four squares to an inch.

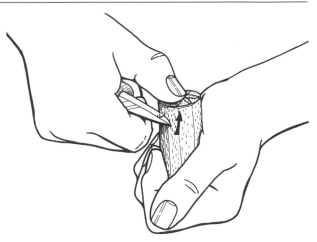

13-1 *Use the compass to draw out the six-point guidelines for the flower motif and to establish the size and position of the dished recess.*

13-3 *Pare the wood to a round section. The best procedure is first to trim the end waste down to the line of the drawn circle, and then skim the rest of the waste down to match.*

ROUGHING OUT THE FLOWER

3. Take the block of wood for the flower and start by swiftly clearing the rough so that you have the round section. The best way of working is to butt the length of wood hard up against the bench hook, and use the small plane (*see* 13-2). And so you continue, planing and turning, planing and turning, until you are left with a cylinder a little under 1 inch in diameter.

4. When you have achieved the cylindrical blank, take the knife and trim the wood down to a smooth finish. Work with a careful, thumb-braced paring stroke (*see* 13-3).

13-2 *Arrange the work-piece hard against the bench hook—so that the surface to be planed stands higher than the stop. This way, you can follow through with the plane.*

5. Still working with the knife, run a stop-cut around the flower end of the cylinder—at a point about 1/8 inch down from the top—and then carry on whittling and reducing the wood below the line, until the wood runs down in a smooth curve to a stalk diameter of about 5/8-inch diameter (*see* 13-4, left).

6. When you are pleased with the curved shape that undercuts around what will be the edge of the petals, move to the drill press and run a 1/8-inch-diameter hole down into the center of the flower. Sink the hole in to a depth of about 1 inch (*see* 13-4, right).

7. Now take the gouge and spoon out the top of the flower—from the edge in towards the drilled hole—so as to make a dished area. Aim for a saucer-like depression that runs down to about a depth of 1/4 inch at its center (*see* the working drawings, bottom-right cross section).

DISHING THE RECESS & DETAILING THE FLOWER PETALS

8. Having first set the 3-inch-diameter circle out on the wood that goes to make the door, drawer, or whatever, move to the drill press and sink a 5/8-inch-diameter hole down through the center of the circle.

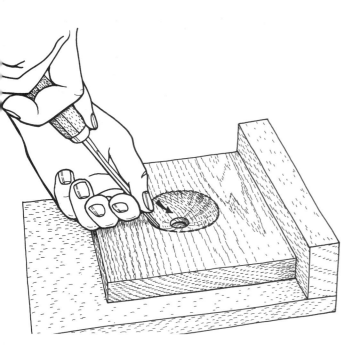

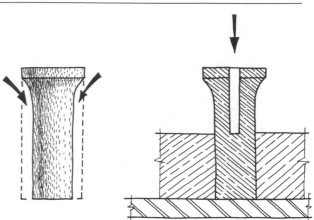

13-4 (Left) Aim for a straight-rimmed trumpet-like section—with a nice crisp curve running down from the rim to the stalk.
(Right) Hold the flower secure in a piece of waste wood, and run a 1/8-inch-diameter hole down through the center.

9. Butt the workpiece hard up against the bench hook stop, then take the gouge and cut from the circle line down-and-in, towards the center. Work systematically around and around the circle until the thickness of wood showing around the edge of the drilled hole is reduced to about 1/8 inch (*see* 13-5). Though you will find it hard going at first, the good news is that by the time you reach a depth of, say, 1/4 inch, you will be able to reduce the effort by levering the tool against the edge of the dish.

10. Plug the flower knob in the hole and see how the two component parts come together. Aim for dished forms—on the flower and the base board—that look as if they come from the same genetic stock.

11. Take the knife and—using the points made by the initial six-point design as a guide—cut the three little nicks that define the petals.

13-5 Use the gouge to scoop out the hollow/recess. Work gradually around and around so as to achieve a uniform dish shape.

13-6 Use the points made by the compass to divide the circumference into three equal parts; then cut these in with the knife. Be careful not to twist the knife into the end grain.

13-7 Having first looked at the working drawings to see how the three component parts relate to each other, cut a little pin to fit in the center of the flower—a pin of a contrasting color.

Widen and model the nicks so as to give the petals their characteristic shape (*see* 13-6).

12. Variously adjust the length and diameter of the flower stalk, so that the flower head is just about flush with the face of the door/drawer front.

13. Take the scrap of wood that you intend using for the flower center, and trim and sand it down so that it is a tight push-fit in the 1/8-inch-diameter hole; then use the knife to round over the little ball head. Aim to have the ball raised slightly above the level of the flower. Aim for a shape that looks a bit like a fat golf tee (*see* 13-7).

14. Finally, having first rubbed the whole works down to a smooth finish, cut, glue, and fit the center in the flower, and the flower in the dished recess.

AFTERTHOUGHTS

• If you enjoy whittling and carving, then you must get yourself a good tool kit. For a good start-up kit you need: a Swedish sloyd knife, a small shallow-sweep straight gouge, and a V-section tool. And of course, once you are up and running, then you can search out and select single tools to suit your needs.

• If you like the notion of simple, naïve whittled and carved knobs, then you need to visit a museum and get to see the entire range of folk art woodcarving: European, Japanese, Chinese, and Indonesian.

• If you intend making a flower knob for a large, heavy drawer, then it might be a good idea to have a long stem that goes through the recessed board, and wedge or pin the stem from the back.

• Project 14 •

Turned Bun Knob

Most of us are familiar with the turned bun knob. You may not know it by that name, and you may not have given it any thought, but nevertheless you will almost certainly know and recognize the form. We say this because just about every piece of ordinary nineteenth-century furniture that you ever did see—chests of drawers, cupboards, wardrobes, and such like—all have bun handles. Of all the turned knobs, the bun form is the most commonplace.

Have a look at the project pictures below and the working drawings on page 86. Consider how this project requires the use of a lathe fitted with a relatively large size chuck. As with most of the turned projects, we use an old Harrison Jubilee lathe and an engineer's four-jaw chuck.

As to the question of why bun type knobs have long been so popular, it's not so difficult to figure out: The rounded bun form just asks to be grasped. The shape invites the hand.

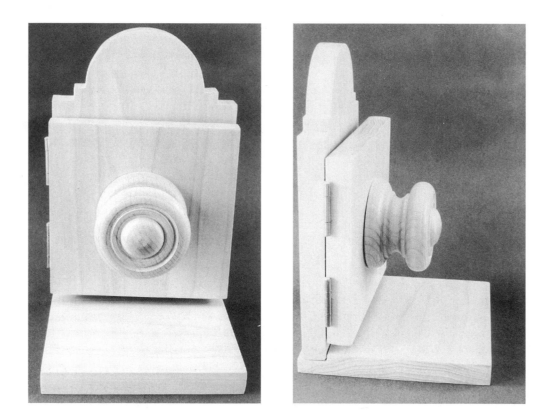

Project pictures—the finished project.

There are many design possibilities that spring directly from the classic bun form.

As to the choice of wood, the big, bold shape and size of the bun knob are such that you can use just about any wood that takes your fancy. Of course the wood needs to be easy to turn, and, yes, you don't want to finish up with a knob that is unduly knotty or one that is likely to split. But that apart, anything goes. I personally favor using traditional woods like lime, beech, pine, sycamore, box, cherry, and maple. We chose to use maple.

WOOD LIST
• A length of 3 1/2 x 3 1/2-inch-square section of wood—a 4-inch length for each knob you want to make

TOOLS & MATERIALS
• A lathe fitted with a four-jaw chuck
• A set of turning tools that includes: a gouge, a parting tool, a round-nosed scraper, and a skew chisel
• A pencil, ruler, and a pair of dividers
• A good sharp knife for general tidying up and trimming—we use a Swedish sloyd knife
• A sheet each of work-out and tracing paper
• All the usual workshop tools and materials . . . sandpaper, PVA glue, dividers, scissors, etc.

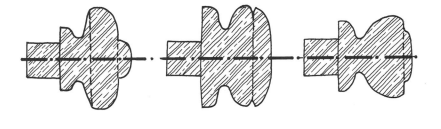

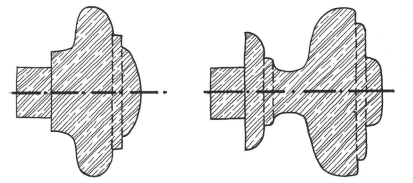

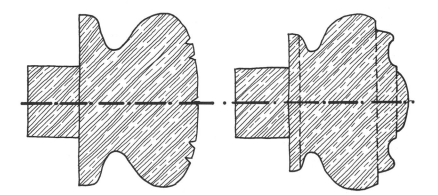

Inspirational designs.
Seven variations on the classic bun form—as seen in cross-section side view.

85

CONSTRUCTION STAGES

Turning the Cylinder & Setting Out the Step-Offs

1. Having selected your wood, and set out your tools, and run through the pre-switch-on checklist that relates to lathe usage, take your chosen length of wood, fix the end center points by drawing crossed diagonals, and mount it securely on the lathe.

2. With the wood well secured, take the gouge and turn the wood down to a clean diameter of 3 inches. While you are at this stage, swiftly turn the first inch of the end down to a diameter of 1 inch—meaning the end nearest to the tail stock. It's important that the diameters be correct, so make repeated checks along the way (*see* 14-1).

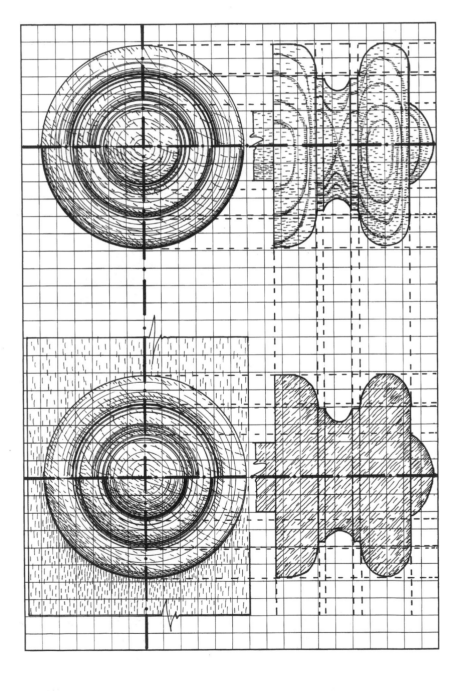

SPECIAL TIP
If you are new to wood-turning, then you will, like as not, be making a good many of your fancy cuts with one or other of the scrapers, rather than the sharp edge-cutting tools. Certainly this is in many ways the best way forward if you are a nervous beginner—but be mindful that a scraped finish will fall a long way short of a finish that has been worked with the skew chisel and the gouge.

Working drawings—at a grid scale of four squares to an inch. Note how this classic bun form is more or less square in proportion—it is about 3 inches in diameter and about 3 inches from front to back.

3. When you have achieved the basic blank, take the dividers and—starting from the tail stock end—mark out the step-offs: 1 inch, 5/8 inch, 3/8 inch, 3/4 inch, 5/16 inch, and 1/4 inch for parting off (*see* 14-2). Note that the last 1/4 inch is for parting waste.

SINKING THE WASTE & TURNING THE BASIC PROFILE

4. Take the parting tool and sink the main areas of waste. Sink the central, 3/8-inch-wide step-off in to a depth of about 5/8 inch—so that you are left with a core diameter of no less than 1 1/2 inches. Check the core diameter with the dividers.

5. Rerun the sinking with the other 3/8-inch step-off, only this time lower the waste by about 1 3/4 inches—so that you are left with a core diameter of 1 1/4 inches (*see* 14-3).

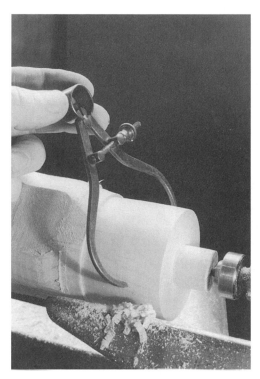

14-1 Check the diameter with the calipers.

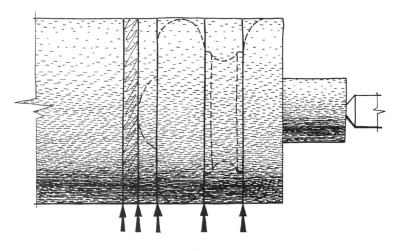

14-2 Use the dividers to mark out all the step-offs that go to make up the design.

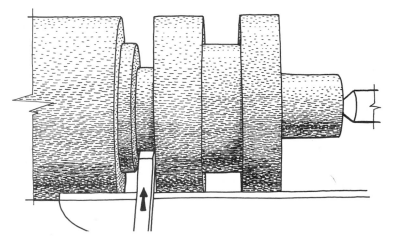

14-3 (Right) Use the parting tool to sink the main areas of waste.

6. When you are happy that all is correct and as described, then take the small gouge or maybe the round-nosed scraper, and turn the sharp shoulders down to nice, rounded curves (*see* 14-4). While you are at it, cut back the waste and use the skew chisel to rough out what will be the decorative button at the front of the bun (*see* 14-4).

7. Don't worry too much at this stage about trying to work to a measured finish, just make sure that the curves are smooth and well balanced, and that the vertical face at the back of the bun—the face that is eventually going to butt up against the piece of furniture—is at right angles to the tenon.

MODELING THE DETAILS & FINISHING

8. Having achieved the basic bun form, then part it off in readiness for the final detailing and finishing.

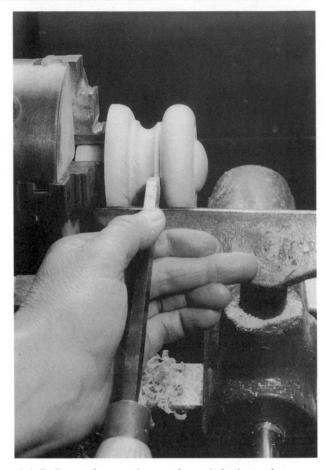

14-5 Run the parting tool straight into the curve so as to create the characteristic square step details.

14-4 Turn the shoulders down—working from high to low wood—until you achieve the nicely balanced and rounded form.

9. With the workpiece mounted securely in the jaws of the chuck—by its tenon—move the tail stock out of the way and reposition the tool rest so that you can approach the bun front-on.

10. Use the skew chisel to first tidy up the central button and to cut the decorative beads, then reset the tool rest so that it is at the side of the lathe and use the parting tool to cut the two steps (*see* 14-5).

11. Finally, swiftly rub the knob down with a fold of fine-grade sandpaper, burnish the whole works with beeswax . . . and then on to the next knob.

AFTERTHOUGHTS

- If you enjoy woodturning, then we would strongly recommend that you get yourself a full facemask-cum-respirator. This piece of equipment not only protects you from all the potentially harmful fine dust, it also offers impact protection from flying wood chips and the like.

- If you like the idea of making bun knobs, but want to go for another design, then visit a furniture museum and get to see the knobs that were made by the nineteenth-century turners.

- If you want to make knobs that will eventually get to be varnished or oiled, then leave out the beeswax stage.

- If you want a set of knobs, then the best way to go is to turn them all at once—all of a piece—from the same length of wood, like a string of beads.

- If you are looking to attach a knob to a drawer front, then you had best wedge it from inside the drawer.

• Project 15 •
Turned Mushroom Knob

Of all the turned knobs, the classic mushroom form—much beloved by the Shakers and the English Arts & Crafts furniture makers—is, at one and the same time, one of the most attractive knobs and among the easiest to make. Have a look at the project pictures below and the working drawings and note how this project requires the use of a lathe fitted with a chuck.

We use an old Harrison Jubilee lathe and an engineer's four-jaw chuck.

Study the mushroom knobs and see how their success has to do with their simple, uncomplicated, no-messing-around shape—just the mushroom top, a flared stem, the shoulder, and no fussing. There are many design possibilities on the same theme.

Project pictures—the finished project.

As to the choice of wood, much depends on the size and the detailing of the knob that you have in mind. Of course the wood needs to be relatively easy to turn, but you can go for just about anything from lime, beech, and pine, to sycamore, cherry, or whatever—as long as it is tight grained and free from knots. We have chosen to use European box.

WOOD LIST

- A length of 1 1/2 x 1 1/2-inch-square section of wood—a 2-inch length for each handle that you want to make

TOOLS & MATERIALS

- A lathe fitted with a four-jaw chuck
- A set of turning tools that includes: a parting tool, a round-nosed scraper, a gouge, and a skew chisel
- A pencil, ruler, and a pair of dividers
- A good sharp knife for general tidying up—we use a Swedish sloyd knife
- A sheet each of work-out and tracing paper
- All the usual workshop tools and materials . . . sandpaper, PVA glue, dividers, scissors, etc.

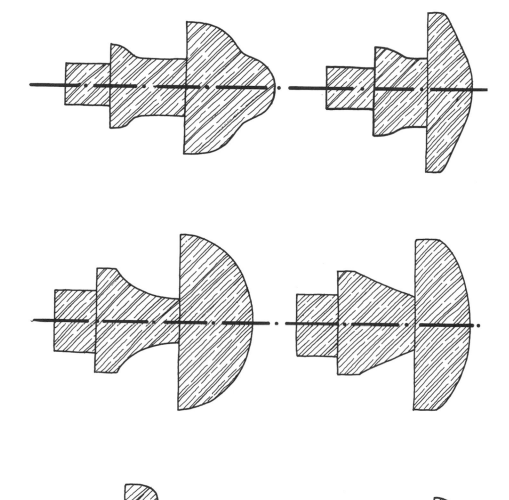

Inspirational designs. Seven variations on the mushroom theme—as seen in cross-section side view.

CONSTRUCTION STAGES

Turning the Cylinder & Setting Out the Step-Offs

1. When you have selected your wood and generally made sure that you and the lathe are in good order and ready for the task in hand, take the wood and establish the end center points by drawing crossed diagonals.

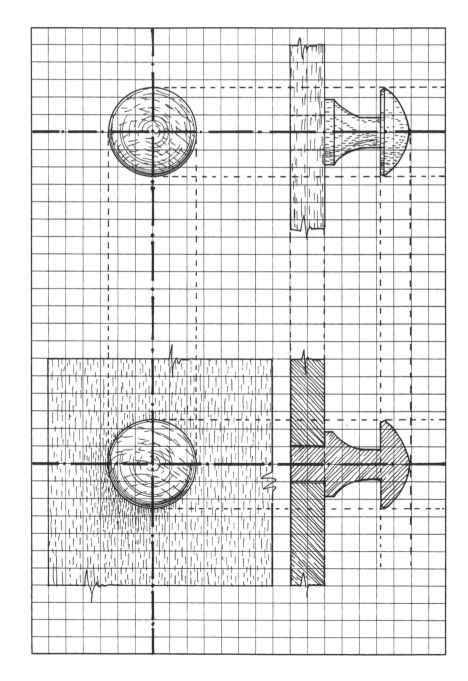

Working drawings—at a grid scale of four squares to an inch.

Have a good long look at the section detail at bottom right, and see how the form is both subtle and functional. Remember, if you change and/or reduce the size of the knob, there needs to be a good length of neck to allow room for your fingers.

15-1 Use the dividers to set the step-offs out with scored lines. Note that the broken lines show how the step-offs relate to the finished form.

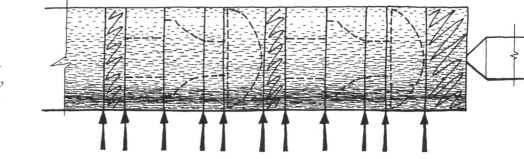

2. Mount the wood on the lathe and swiftly turn it down to a 1 3/8-inch-diameter cylinder.

3. Having first studied the working drawings thoroughly, take the ruler and dividers and set out all the step-offs that go to make up the design. Working along from the tail stock end, allow a small amount of tail stock waste and then set out the sequence: 1/2 inch, 1/4 inch, 1/2 inch, and 1/2 inch—repeating the sequence for each knob that you want to turn (*see 15-1*).

NOTE

Just in case you don't know, many woodturners describe their turnings in terms that have to with the human body. For example, a turning like a chess piece or a vase might have a head, a neck, a belly, a waist, a foot, and so on.

TURNING OFF THE PROFILE

4. Shade in the areas of waste, organize your working area so that the drawings and the calipers are close at hand, then take the parting tool and sink the 1/4-inch band of waste between the two knobs, as well as the waste at each stem or neck (*see 15-2*).

15-2 Use the parting tool to swiftly sink the waste. Make sure that the height of the tool rest allows for the thickness of the tool.

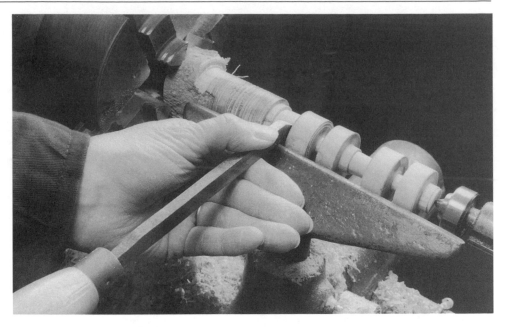

15-3 Set the bevel down on the work-piece, gently raise the handle until the cutting edge begins to bite, and then advance the cut.

SPECIAL TIP
Although I have chosen to turn the tenon down to 1/2-inch diameter—to fit my range of drill bits—you will of course need to size your tenon to fit your own drill bits.

15-4 Saw the turning down—so that there is a stub of waste at the top of the mushroom.

5. Still working with the parting tool—turn the tenon/dowel end of each knob down to a diameter of 1/2 inch (*see* 15-3). Go at it nice and slowly so that you don't knock the workpiece off center.

6. With the bulk of the waste cleared with the parting tool, then take the round-nosed gouge or the scraper and turn down the shoulder and the curved shape that runs from the shoulder to the neck.

7. When you have turned your string of knobs, done your best to make certain that they are well matched, and sized the tenons so that they are a tight push-fit in a 1/2-inch-diameter hole, then remove the workpiece from the lathe and saw the turning down into the component parts (*see* 15-4).

15-5 Mount the knob in the chuck and—working over the bed of the lathe—bring it to a good finish.

WORKING OVER THE BED OF THE LATHE & FINISHING

8. Secure the knob in the chuck, move the tail stock back out of the way, and bring the tool rest up to the workpiece so that you can approach it end-on.

9. Double-check that the workpiece is well mounted in the chuck, then take the tool of your choice—a round-nosed scraper or the skew chisel would be appropriate—and turn the top of the mushroom down to a smooth-curved profile (*see* 15-5). Go at it very gently, all the while being very careful not to let your tool snag the workpiece off center.

10. Use the graded sandpapers to rub the knob down to a good finish. Pay particular attention to the difficult-to-reach face between the back of the mushroom and the neck.

11. Last of all, use some beeswax and a fluff-free cotton cloth to burnish the knob to a high shine.

AFTERTHOUGHTS

• Although my four-jaw chuck was expensive—it cost a quarter of the price of my lathe—it is the best way I know of making sure that the workpiece is held secure.

• Don't be fooled into thinking that a three-jawed chuck is as good as a four-jaw. Think about it—you can't hold and center a square-section piece of wood in a three-jaw chuck!

• Remember, if you are a beginner, that the ideal is to make the turning without recourse to using sandpaper. If you and the tools are sharp, then you won't need sandpaper!

• It needs emphasizing that the choice of wood is all-important—you must use a tight-grained wood free of splits and knots.

• Because the top surface of the knob is end grain, it needs to be well sealed with polish before it's removed from the lathe. If you fail to do this, then the end grain will swiftly become discolored and soiled.

• Project 16 •

Laminated Turned Knob

Over the last few years, woodturners have become more and more interested in laminating. It's a beautifully ingenious and exciting technique; all you do is make a sandwich or lamination of various contrasting woods, stick them together to make a square section, and then work through the turning procedures as usual. The clever bit, the good-fun bit, has to do with building more complex secondary laminations that result in highly patterned turned forms.

Have a look at the project pictures below and the working drawings and note how the simplest primary two-color arrangement of the wood results in a turned design that is surprising in its complexity. Study the inspirational designs for more complicated laminations. As to what happens when these arrangements are turned, that's for you to find out!

As usual, we use an old Harrison Jubilee lathe fitted with an engineer's four-jaw chuck.

As to the choice of wood, it's a little more complicated, because while you need wood colors that are nicely contrasting, you also need woods that are similar in grain and texture. For example, you might have a piece of dark cherry with a piece of creamy lime, or a piece of red

Project pictures—the finished project.

plum and white holly, and so on. We have gone for medium-light ash and a piece of dark brown driftwood mahogany. Although we were happy to use the mahogany—because it was old and salvaged—we weren't too sure about the ragged texture of the ash. However, they set each other off nicely and were easy to turn.

WOOD LIST
- Three 12-inch lengths of 2-inch-wide mahogany about 3/8 inch thick
- Four 12-inch lengths of 2-inch-wide ash about 1/8 to 3/16 inch thick Note: All the wood needs to be well planed to a uniform thickness.

TOOLS & MATERIALS
- A lathe fitted with a four-jaw chuck
- A set of turning tools that includes: a gouge, a parting tool, a round-nosed scraper, and a skew chisel
- A pencil, ruler, and a pair of dividers
- A good sharp knife for general tidying up—we use a Swedish sloyd knife
- A sheet each of work-out and tracing paper
- A good number of small-size clamps
- All the usual workshop tools and materials . . . sandpaper, PVA glue, dividers, scissors, etc.

Inspirational designs. Various patterns for gluing up the laminations. Note that the circle will give you some idea of how the turning will look in cross section.

CONSTRUCTION STAGES

Laminating

1. Take your chosen wood and check it over for potential problems—splits, dead knots, and so forth—and have a trial dry-run arrangement and clamping (*see* 16-1). Select your clamps and two lengths of waste wood, make sure you have plenty of glue, and generally decide on the order of work.

2. Having first pencil-labeled all the mating faces—so that you know precisely what goes where and how—smear glue on all of faces and clamp them up (*see* 16-2). Keep in mind that it's most important that all of the mating faces be completely flush and well glued. If you make a poor joint, then it will show in the piece as a cavity once you start the turning.

> **SPECIAL TIP**
> Keeping in mind that gluing and clamping are by their very nature a sticky, messy business, it is always a good idea to plan everything in advance. We always have a trial dry run—planning everything from the order of clamps, to where in the workshop we're going to leave the arrangement while the glue is setting.

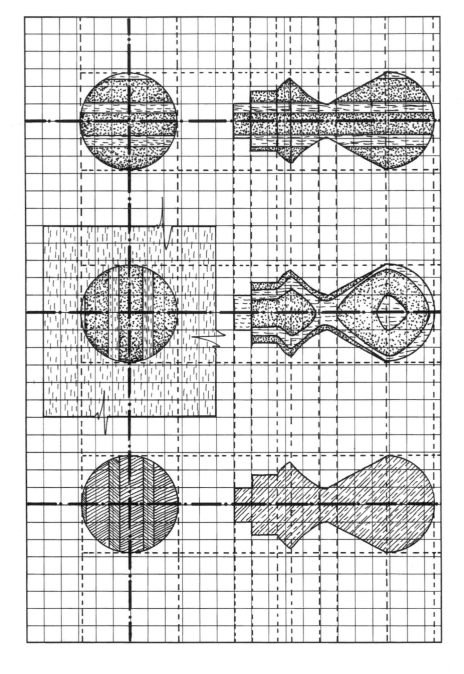

Working drawings—at a grid scale of four squares to an inch.

Note how quite subtle changes in the turned form completely change the shape of the laminated contour patterns.

3. When the glue is dry, use a bench plane or rasp to swiftly clean up the faces and cut the block down to a rough square section.

SPECIAL TIP

If you are working with a small amount of special wood and/or you are worried about the lathe centers doing damage to the ends of your wood, then you could glue a piece of waste wood at either end of the work-piece to act as a buffer and strengthener.

TURNING THE CYLINDER & SETTING OUT THE STEP-OFFS

4. Establish the end centers by drawing crossed diagonals and mount the blank securely on the lathe (*see* 16-3). It has to be right the first time around, so make sure that everything is good and secure.

5. With the wood well mounted, first use a large gouge to swiftly clear the rough; then use the large skew chisel to turn it down to a 1 1/2-inch-diameter cylinder (*see* 16-4).

16-1 *Plane your chosen laminations to a good smooth finish and stack them in the gluing order.*

16-3 *Spend time making sure that the workpiece is well mounted on the lathe.*

16-2 *Sandwich the stack between waste wood, and clamp up. Be generous with both the glue and the clamps.*

16-4 *When you are using the skew chisel, have the tool rest set up high and close so that you can work from above.*

16-5 *Set out all the step-offs that make up the design.*

16-6 *When you come to lower the waste for the tenons, make sure that their diameter matches up with one of your drill sizes.*

16-7 *If and when you come to use the scraper, then be sure to have the tool rest set so that the scraper makes a high cut. If you have the tool rest too low, the scraper might tear the workpiece off the lathe.*

6. Take the ruler and dividers and set out all the step-offs that make up the design. Working along from the tail stock end of the workpiece, allow a small amount of waste and then about 1 1/2 inches for the knob proper, 3/4 inch for the shoulder, 3/4 inch for the return, and 3/4 inch for the two tenons. Then reverse, and repeat the step-offs for the rest of the other knob. Pencil-shade the areas of waste and the tenons (*see* 16-5).

7. With all the guidelines in place, take the parting tool and lower the various step-offs to the required core diameters (*see* 16-6).

TURNING OFF THE PROFILE

8. Having first studied the working drawings—so that you have a clear image of all the contours and profiles that make up the design—take the round-nosed scraper and round over the half-sphere ends. Work in the direction of the grain—from high to low wood. Run the curve from the meridian line down towards what will eventually be the center of the ball end.

9. Take the parting tool, or the round-nosed scraper, and swiftly cut the angled line that runs from the meridian line down into the waist. Rerun this procedure for both knobs (*see* 16-7).

10. And so you continue, turning the curved waist, turning the angled shoulders, until you have what you consider is a well-matched pair of knobs (*see* 16-8).

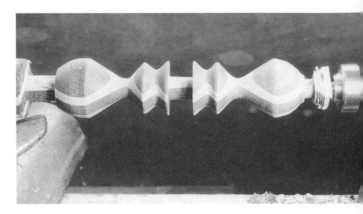

16-8 *Note the extra flanges just above the tenon, which needed to be changed.*

SPECIAL TIP

If you compare our working drawings with the photographs, you will see that the photographs show the knob having an extra flare towards the base. What happened was that right at the last moment, we decided that because we needed longer tenons, and because one of the flares was starting to split, we would slightly modify the design. The point is: Don't slavishly copy our designs and/or admit defeat if something goes wrong. Always be ready to change the design to suit your own needs.

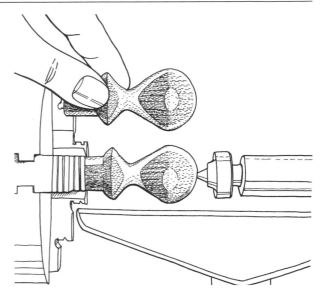

16-9 Having first switched off the power, make repeated comparisons to ensure a good match.

WORKING OVER THE BED OF THE LATHE & FINISHING

11. When you are happy with the string of shapes that make up the design, rub it down with fine-grade sandpaper and remove it from the lathe. Use the fine saw to cut away the waste and separate the two knobs.

12. Secure the knob in the chuck—by the tenon—move the tail stock back out of the way, and bring the tool rest up to the workpiece so that you can approach it end-on. Use the round-nosed scraper or the skew chisel to turn the stub of parting waste down to the level of the curve. Go at it very gently, being careful that you don't jolt the knob off center.

13. Finally, wind the tail stock up so that the workpiece is just supported at the center (*see* 16-9) and then work through the finishing procedures of sanding, waxing and burnishing. If it's important that the two knobs be a well-matched pair, then now is the time to make comparisons and adjustments.

AFTERTHOUGHTS

- It's worth repeating that our four-jaw chuck is without doubt a wonderfully useful piece of equipment. It was expensive—but then again it's a very easy way of swiftly turning down from a square section. There's no need for any preliminary turning or fussing about. We just secure the wood in the jaws of the chuck and we're off!

- If, like us, you happen to make a mess-up and some part of the turning is damaged, have a quick scream and then get back in there and make whatever changes will rescue your work. Use the mess-up as a challenge.

- The mahogany was a piece of salvaged driftwood—almost certainly a piece of rail from an old dinghy. At our reckoning it must be at least fifty years old. If you get the chance to use salvaged wood, then go for it.

• Project 17 •

Turned Acorn Knob

Woodworkers have long been fascinated by acorn imagery! We don't really know the reasons for this phenomenon. Maybe it has to do with the ancient link-up between oak trees and tree worship, or perhaps it's simply that acorns are such an attractive and complete form, who knows? All we do know for sure is that there are carved acorns in English churches, acorn finials on furniture, acorn motifs on Arts & Crafts fur-

niture, and so on. Then again, there are also all manner of closely related fruit and bud forms used on furniture. And of course, once you are tuned into looking for woodworked acorns and the like, you will begin to see them almost everywhere you care to look!

Study the project pictures below and the working drawings, and consider how this project requires the use of a lathe fitted with a chuck. As

Project pictures—the finished project.

we have done with most of the turned projects, we use an old Harrison Jubilee lathe and an engineer's four-jaw chuck.

There are many design possibilities—as you can see below—that relate to the acorn, inasmuch as they all draw their inspiration from plant bud and fruit forms.

As to the choice of wood, you can't do better than go for a hardwood like maple, sycamore, lime, or any of the fruit woods.

WOOD LIST

- A length of 1 1/2 x 1 1/2-inch-square section of wood—a 4-inch length for each knob that you want to make

TOOLS & MATERIALS

- A lathe fitted with a four-jaw chuck
- A set of turning tools that includes: a gouge, a parting tool, a round-nosed scraper, and a skew chisel
- A pencil, ruler, and a pair of dividers
- A good sharp knife for general tidying up and trimming—we use a Swedish sloyd knife
- A sheet each of work-out and tracing paper
- All the usual workshop tools and materials . . . sandpaper, PVA glue, dividers, scissors, etc.

SPECIAL TIP
Although we don't perhaps use all the tools and materials listed in this project—such as the paper and the scissors—you might well want to cut out a paper profile or whatever. Moreover, it's always a good idea to make sure that all the makings are close at hand.

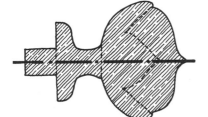
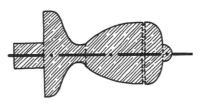

Inspirational designs.
Eight variations on the classic nut, fruit, bud form—as seen in cross-section side view.

CONSTRUCTION STAGES

Turning the Cylinder & Setting Out the Step-Offs

1. When you are ready to start—with your lathe nicely tuned and your tools at the ready—take your chosen length of wood, and draw crossed diagonals across the ends to establish the end center points.

2. Mount the workpiece on the lathe, and make adjustments—bringing the tool rest up to the work. Then take the gouge and swiftly turn the wood down to the largest possible round section.

3. Once you have achieved a smooth cylinder, then take the dividers and, using the drawn image for reference, mark in all the step-offs that make up the design.

SPECIAL TIP

Because woodturning is potentially dangerous, it's most important that you are alert, the machine is in good order, and your whole working environment is in harmony with what you are preparing to do. No flapping cuffs or loose hair, no out-of-control children, no ringing phones, no broken tools or suspect machinery. For safety's sake everything needs to be just so. We're not being fussy. It's just good safe working practice! But of course children should be encouraged to join in the fun; just make sure that they watch at a safe distance!

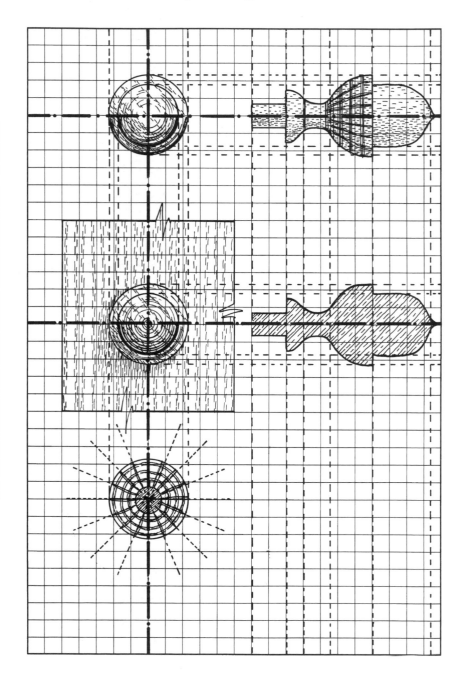

Working drawings—at a grid scale of four squares to an inch.

4. Based on our two-acorn arrangement, and working from left to right along the wood, allow: about 1 inch for head stock parting off, 1 inch for the rounded part of the first acorn, 3/4 inch for the cap, 3/8 inch for the stem, 1/4 inch for the stepped flange, 1/2 inch for the tenon or dowel fixing. Then reverse, and repeat all the measurements for the other acorns (*see* 17-1). It's a good idea to shade in selected areas so that you can see what you are trying to achieve.

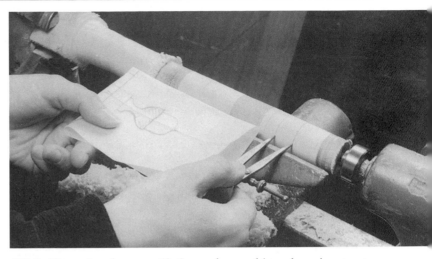

17-1 Transfer the step-offs from the working drawing to the wood.

SPECIAL TIP

In the interests of efficiency and safety, it's most important that the tool rest always be as close as possible to the workpiece. Always aim to have the tool rest or fulcrum arranged so that only the tip of the tool seesaws between the T-rest and the work.

LOWERING THE WASTE & MODELING

5. When you have achieved the cylinder—all clearly marked out with the dividers and pencil—take the parting tools and the calipers and lower the waste. The procedure is: Read off the required core diameter with the calipers—that is, set the calipers so that they relate to your working drawings—and then lower the waste with the parting tool until the calipers' points just slip over the diameter (*see* 17-2).

6. Rerun the procedure with the calipers and the parting tool until each step-off core diameter matches up with the working drawing (*see* 17-3).

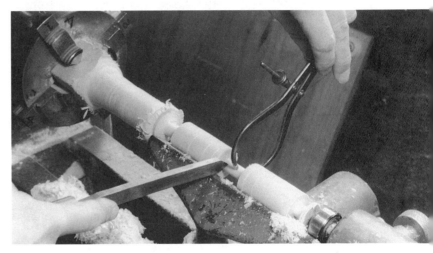

17-2 The core diameter is achieved when the tips of the calipers just slide free.

17-3 See how the mirror-image, back-to-back arrangement of the two knobs is an aid to achieving a matched pair.

7. When you have turned down the core diameters, take the round-nosed scraper and set to work turning the acorn cap and stem to shape. Go at it nice and slowly, down and around the cap (*see* 17-4), along the stem, and around the curve of the base. Aim for a smooth-curved valley.

8. Rerun more or less the same procedure when you come to shaping the smooth round-ness of the nut (*see* 17-5). Use the skew chisel to round over the end of the nut—either use the heel to cut, or the point to scrape.

SPECIAL TIP

When you come to rounding over the ends of the nut-and so consequently reduce the diameter of the parting-off waste—it's best to work first on the acorn nearest the tail stock. This order of work ensures that the bulk of wood between the head stock and the first acorn is left in place until the last moment.

17-4 Be careful, when you are running the tool down into the dip of the stem, not to allow the tip of the tool to slide under the workpiece.

9. Last of all, reduce the diameter of the tenon stalk—that is, the end that is going to be dowel-tenon fixed into your cupboard or drawer—so that it matches up with one of your drill bit sizes. You'd best go for 3/8 or 1/2 inch.

CHUCK WORK & WHITTLING

10. When you are happy with the forms, remove the workpiece from the lathe and use a fine blade saw to separate the acorns.

11. Mount the acorn in the jaws of the chuck, and push the tail stock back out of the way. Then reposition the tool rest over the bed of the lathe so that you will be able to approach the acorn end-on.

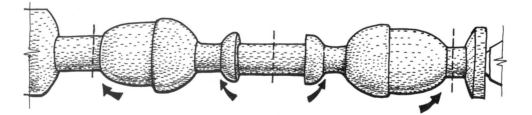

17-5 Very gently reduce the parting-off waste and turn the round profiles down to a smooth finish.

17-6 Make certain that the workpiece is held secure and true. If you are worried that you might knock it off center, then wind the tail stock up for additional support.

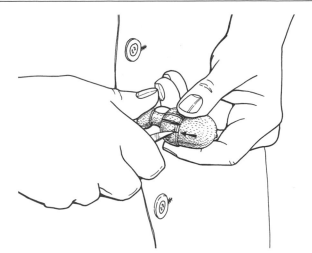

17-7 For optimum control, have your elbows tucked hard into your sides, and work with a two-handed thumb-braced paring cut.

12. Use the tools of your choice to turn the parting-off stub down to a nicely rounded peaked finish (*see* 17-6). Be very careful that you don't knock the acorn off center.

13. When you have achieved the two acorns—all turned, sanded, and polished—take the knife and work around the cap so as to cut a series of shallow grooves that radiate out from the stem (*see* 17-7). The best procedure for spacing the grooves is first to quarter the total, and then halve the quarter, and so on—refer to the bottom left of the working drawings.

14. Finally, run three grooved cuts around the cap, so that you finish up with a pattern of diminishing squares (*see* 17-8).

AFTERTHOUGHTS

• If you are working on a borrowed lathe and are thinking about getting a machine of your own, then I would recommend that you go for the biggest and best machine you can afford. And don't think that small items are best turned on a small lathe—not a bit of it! The bigger the lathe, the more control.

17-8 Each V-section groove is achieved with three cuts—a straight-down stop-cut to establish the depth of the groove, a slanting cut to one side to remove half the waste, and a final slanting cut to the other side to complete the V-trench.

• If you like the idea of making acorns and plan to turn something bigger, then how about turning a massive pineapple finial knob for your staircase newel post?

• Project 18 •

Turned & Recessed Knob

Study the project pictures below and the working drawings and note how this project requires the use of a 2 1/8-inch-diameter Forstner bit to sink the recess, plus a lathe fitted with a good-size chuck. Though we use a large-size four-jaw engineer's chuck, this is not to say that you can't achieve the knob by working between centers; it's just that the four-jaw chuck makes the whole turning procedure that much easier.

Have a look at the inspirational drawings—the opposite page of detailed cross sections—and note how many possible variations there are on the turned-plug-in-a-drilled-hole theme. For example: The turning can be flush with both surfaces, or be standing proud at the front, or have a stepped tenon and be entered in from the back, and so on—there are many options. Note how we have fitted the finished handle so that it stands slightly proud of its setting.

As for the choice of wood, the only critical factor is that the wood must be easy to turn and relatively tight grained. Something like cherry, box, lime, or sycamore is fine. But you do have to be cautious. For example, having decided to

Project pictures—the finished project.

opt for cherry, we mistakenly chose the English variety rather than the American. American cherry turns to a beautiful, dark, hard finish, whereas English cherry is generally light and fluffy and altogether more difficult to turn!

WOOD LIST
- A length of good-to-turn 2 1/2 x 2 1/2-inch-square section wood. You will need to allow 1 1/2-inch lengths for each handle that you want to make

TOOLS & MATERIALS
- A lathe fitted with a four-jaw chuck
- A bench drill press
- A 2 1/8-inch-diameter Forstner drill bit
- A set of woodturning tools that includes: a parting tool, a round-nosed scraper, and a small skew chisel
- A pair of calipers
- A piece of beeswax for burnishing
- A pencil, ruler, and a pair of dividers
- A sheet each of work-out and tracing paper
- All the usual workshop tools and materials . . . sandpaper, PVA glue, dividers, scissors, etc.

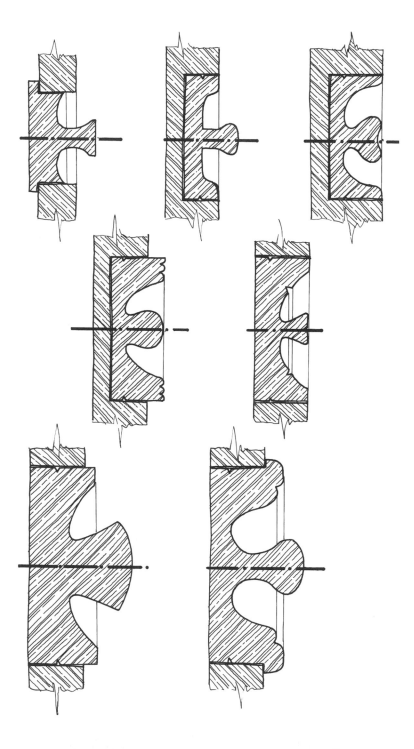

Inspirational designs.
Seven alternatives as seen in cross-section side view.
Note how there are four possible mounting options:
(Top left) The turning with shoulders and entered from the inside of the door;
(Top right) The turning sitting in a blind recess;
(Bottom left) The turning sitting in a through-hole; or
(Bottom right) The turning with shoulders and entered from the front.
Note also how the sides of the turning can be worked with glue grooves.

CONSTRUCTION STAGES

Turning the Blank & Setting Out the Step-Offs

1. When you have studied the project, collected all your tools and materials, and generally sorted out in your own mind precisely how you want the handle to be, then take your chosen square section length of wood and establish the end center points by drawing crossed diagonals.

2. Mount the wood securely on the lathe and swiftly turn it down to a 2 1/4-inch-diameter cylinder. Use the calipers to make sure that the diameter is correct.

3. Working from the tail stock end of the workpiece and allowing for a small length of tail stock waste, take your dividers and set out alternate step-offs at 1 inch and 1/4 inch, 1 inch and 1/4 inch, and so on. Note

that the 1/4-inch step-off might need to be slightly wider to fit your parting tool.

4. Having established the step-offs, take the parting tool and sink them in to a depth of about 1/4 inch (*see* 18-1). If you have done it right, each of the 1/4-inch step-offs should be turned down to a core diameter of about 5/8 to 3/4 inch.

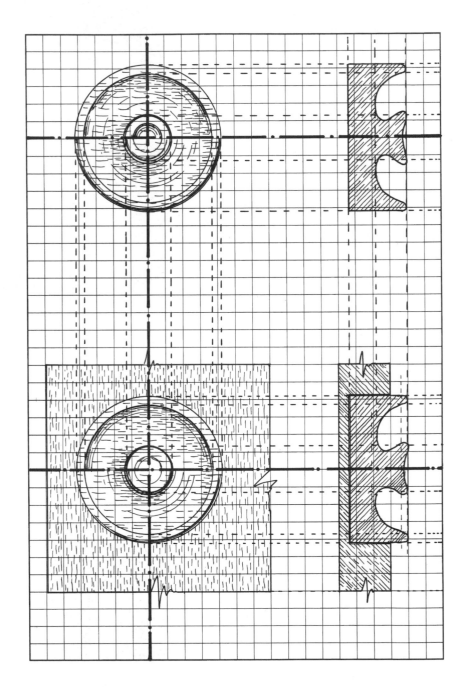

Working drawings—at a grid scale of four squares to an inch.
Note how the turning is mounted in the recess so that the rim stands proud.

WORKING OVER THE BED OF THE LATHE

5. When you have turned the cylinder to size, take it off the lathe and saw it down so that you have a number of handle blanks.

SPECIAL TIP

If you are new to woodturning and maybe a bit nervous that the workpiece is going to fly off and do damage, then you can't do better than protect yourself with a full facemask with filter.

6. Mount the blank on the lathe—so that the tenon is captured in the jaws of the chuck—and then push the tail stock back out of the way so that you can approach the workpiece end-face-on.

7. Turn the end face down to a smooth finish, and reduce the diameter so that it is a tight push-fit in a 2 1/8-inch-diameter hole. It's best to run a 2 1/8-inch-diameter hole through a piece of scrap wood and then to make repeated tests along the way (*see* 18-2).

8. Use the dividers to set the face of the turning out with the step-offs that make up the design (*see* 18-3). Have a look at the working drawings and note how the central knob needs to be about 3/4 inch in diameter.

18-3 When you come to mark out the various step-offs on the face of the spinning workpiece, then be sure for safety's sake to mark out the left-hand quadrant—so that the dividers are pushed down and supported on the tool rest.

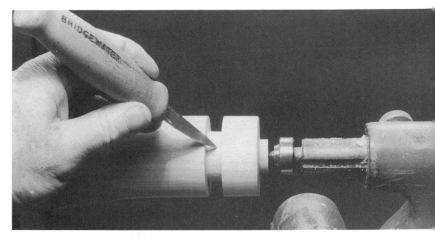

18-1 Make sure that the tenon you propose sinking is as wide as your parting tool.

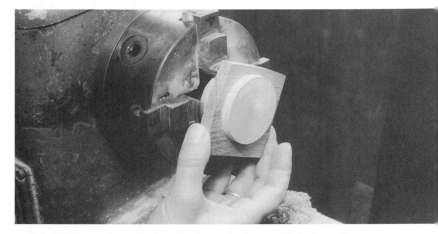

18-2 Reduce the cylinder little by little, until it is a tight push-fit in a 2 1/8-inch-diameter hole.

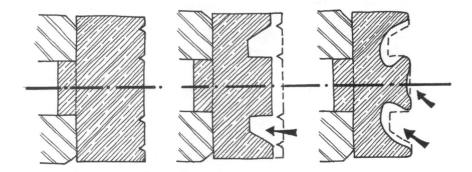

18-4 From left to right—the working sequence.

9. When you have studied the working drawings and set the workpiece out with as many step-off guidelines as you think necessary, then comes the good-fun task of turning the curved profile. The order of work (*see* 18-4, left to right) is:

- Use the parting tool to sink the main areas of waste and to establish the overall shape of the knob and the rim.
- Use the round-nosed scraper to turn the moat-like dip that rings around the knob.
- Use the tools of your choice to detail the center of the knob and the shape of the rim.

10. First, use a small scrap of fine-grade sandpaper to rub the workpiece down (*see* 18-5), and then use the beeswax to burnish the surface to a high-shine finish. Be careful not to get polish on the sides of the turning—that is, the areas that are to be glued.

11. Finally, once you are satisfied that you are completely done with the front side of the workpiece, release it and then reverse it in the chuck so that the tenon is looking out over the bed of the lathe. With the workpiece reversed, then you can turn the back down to a good, slightly concave finish (*see* 18-6).

18-5 Use the fine-grade sandpaper to rub down, and the wax to burnish—all before you reverse the workpiece in the chuck to turn off the tenon.

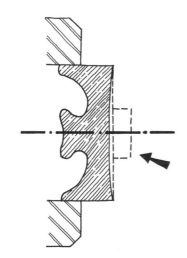

18-6 Turn the back of the workpiece down to a slightly concave finish—so as to ensure that it fits snuggly into the bored recess.

AFTERTHOUGHTS

- If you are perhaps working on a borrowed lathe and are considering buying one of your own, then our best advice is to go for the biggest lathe that you can afford and fit it out with a four-jaw chuck and a tail stock chuck.

- Be warned: A four-jaw chuck needs to be used in conjunction with a guard. Though our guard—removed so that you can see what's going on—is no more than a thin strip of plywood that we arch over the chuck and clamp to the bed, it nicely prevents the left hand from coming into contact with the spinning chuck.

- If and when you come to wax and burnish the spinning workpiece with a cloth, then be sure to make the cloth into a pad, rather than wrap it around your fingers. This way, you won't come to harm if the cloth gets caught up in the chuck.

- If you are worried about the jaws of the chuck marking the workpiece, then wrap it around with masking tape.

• Project 19 •

Lift Latch

Have a look at the project pictures below and the working drawings on page 116 and note how this project might almost be thought of as a universal off-the-shelf kit-type latch. That is to say, the parts are so uniform—almost as if they have been clipped to size and shape on a machine—that they might be modified to suit all manner of lift latch sizes and locations.

Note how this project can be achieved with the minimum of hand tools. All you need are a saw, a drill, a knife, and a mortise gauge for setting out, and you are well away.

Project pictures—the finished project.

Have a look at the inspirational drawings below—and note how many variations there are on the lift latch theme.

As regards the best wood for the job, though it does need to be tight grained and strong along the length of the grain, you can use just about any wood that strikes your fancy. We have gone for English plum for the strips, and white wood dowel for the various pivots and pins—with selected pins being stained black.

WOOD LIST
- A 1/4-inch-thick, 3/4-inch-wide strip, about 14 inches long, for each lift latch that you want to make
- A prepared length of 1/4-inch-diameter dowel about 12 inches long

TOOLS & MATERIALS
- A small brass-backed saw—we used a gent's
- A bench drill press
  - A 1/4-inch-diameter Forstner drill bit
  - A mortise marking gauge
  - A 1/4-inch-wide out-cannel gouge—called out-cannel because the bevel or bezel is on the inside of the curve
  - A small knife for shaping—we use a Swedish sloyd-type knife
  - A quantity of beeswax for burnishing
  - A pencil, ruler, and a pair of dividers
  - A sheet each of work-out and tracing paper
  - All the usual workshop tools and materials . . . sandpaper, PVA glue, dividers, scissors, etc.

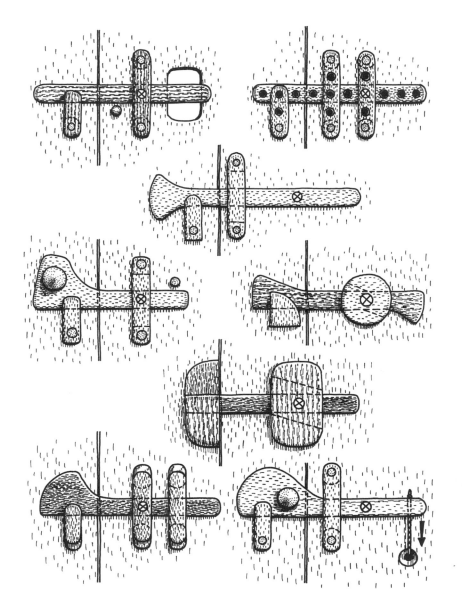

Inspirational designs.
Various alternatives on the lift-latch theme.
Note especially:
(Top left) The one with the pierced hole; and
(Bottom right) The one with the hole and string.
Note that both allow the latch to be lifted from the other side of the door.

CONSTRUCTION STAGES

Marking Out & Drilling

1. Having first brought your tools to good order and checked to make sure that the wood is free from splits and knots, take the marking gauge and set the two pins 3/8 inch apart, the inner pin being 3/8 inch away from the block.

2. Take your chosen prepared wood and run the gauge along one planed edge, so as to strike off two parallel lines (*see* 19-1). Note how the line nearest the edge of the wood is the centerline, and the line farthest away is the cutting line.

3. Run a saw through the cutting line so that you are left with a 3/4-inch-wide strip.

4. Take a break to clear your mind—and refresh your eye by looking at the working drawings. Then take the pencil, ruler, and dividers and set out all the lengths, half-circle ends, and center points that make up the design (*see* 19-2). We recommend that you shade in the waste areas so that they are distinct and the shapes are clear to see.

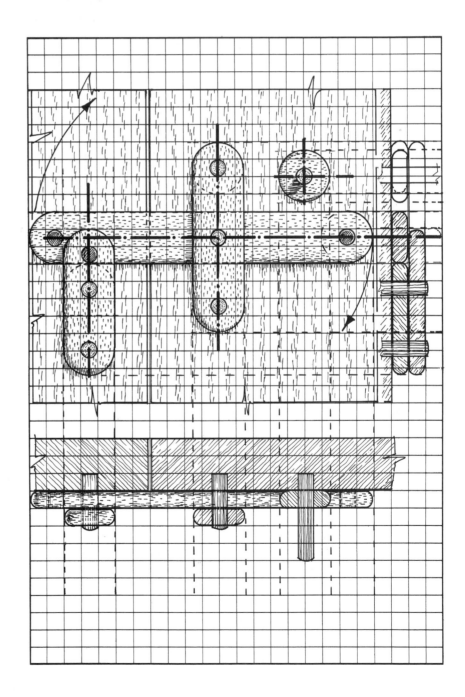

Working drawings—at a grid scale of four squares to an inch.

DRILLING & SHAPING

5. Look over the working drawings once more and carefully check that all of the measurements are correct. Then run 1/4-inch-diameter holes through all the center points; afterwards, saw the strip down into its component parts (*see* 19-3). Keeping in mind that the side of the wood without the centerline is the best face, do your best to ensure that the drill bit leaves a clean exit hole.

6. Now take your knife and round over all the edges and ends—so that all the curves are of more or less 1/4 inch diameter. You should finish up with a total of seven component parts: three little disks or spacers, the main lift latch at about 5 inches long, the cross-latch plate at 2 3/4 inches, the under-latch spacer at 1 5/8 inches, and the catch-latch plate at 2 1/8 inches long (*see* 19-4)—all cut to length, drilled, and swiftly trimmed to shape.

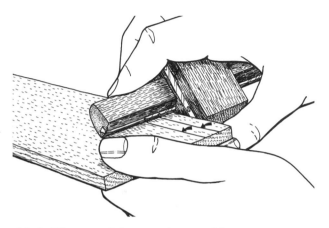

19-1 *The use of the mortise marking gauge ensures that the centerline and the cutting line are parallel—it's a swift and easy way of setting out the wood.*

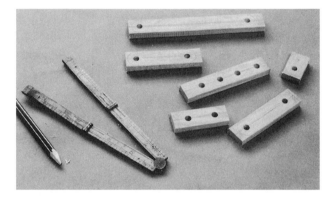

19-3 *Having drilled the holes and cut the strip to size, you could, if you so wish, use a coping-type saw to fret the curved ends to shape. Note that not all the holes have been drilled at this stage— also that the washer's spacers have not as yet been cut.*

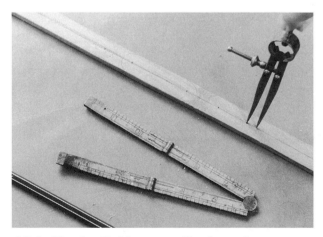

19-2 *Use the dividers to scribe the end curves and to punch the various center points. Don't forget that the side with the scribed centerline will be hidden from view.*

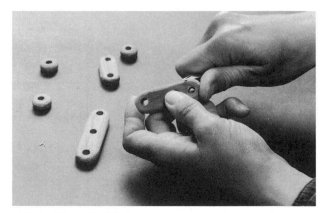

19-4 *Though this is an easy enough procedure, you do have to be very careful that you don't cut your fingers—especially when you are working with the little disk spacers.*

19-5 *If you have in mind making a lot of identical lift catches, then this task could be made much easier by pinning a strip at either side of the workpiece—that is, on the bench hook—so that the workpiece can be slid into place and you could hold the tool with both hands.*

7. Having first made sure that the out-cannel gouge has been honed to a razor sharpness, take the components one at a time, butt them hard up against the bench stop, and use the gouge to trim the edges and ends to a uniform 1/4-inch-diameter section (*see* 19-5). Go at it nice and slowly, all the while being sure to adjust the direction of cut so as to cut in the direction of the grain.

FINISHING & FITTING

8. With all seven of the component parts brought to a crisply rounded edge, take the fine-grade sandpaper and rub the edges down to a smooth finish (*see* 19-6). It's all easy enough, apart from the fact that the little disks are a bit tricky to hold. We found that the best way was to push the disks onto the end of a dowel-like little mushrooms—so at least we had something to grasp.

19-6 *Use the graded sand-papers to rub the wood down to a good finish. Concentrate your efforts on the edges and the best face.*

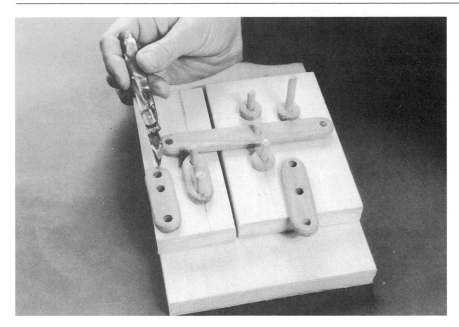

19-7 We decided to go for a subtle decorative effect by having certain holes stopped off with a contrasting wood.

9. When you are happy with the finish, then run the pattern of 1/4-inch-diameter holes in the door, and glue-attach the six dowels in place. Slide and glue the three disk spacers on the dowels, slide and glue the latch-catch spacer plate on its two dowels, set the lift-latch on the pivot dowel—so that it seesaws up and down—and then glue and fit the last two plates in place so that everything is held and contained (*see* 19-7). Note that the holes in the ends of the lift latch and the hole in the top end of the latch catch are stopped off with dowels that have been rubbed flush and picked out with black—to make a decorative feature.

10. Finally, trim back the dowel ends—not forgetting to leave the "stop" dowel longer. Then wax and burnish the whole works to a silky-smooth finish, and the job is done.

AFTERTHOUGHTS

• If you want to make this project really special, then you could use fancy wood for the dowels—boxwood, holly, pear, etc.

• Although overall the project is relatively simple, it is important that the holes be clean-cut. To our way of thinking, the Forstner is the best bit for the task.

• Although this project does more or less relate to a model, the next time around we would have everything relate to the spacing of 3/4 inch. The strip would be 3/4 inch wide, and we would have holes at 3/4-inch intervals along all of the strips. At the end of the day—when we had made decisions as to the pivot and fixing holes—we would give the latch an added look of beauty by filling all the unused holes with contrasting wood.

• Project 20 •
Sliding Bolt Catch

Have a look at the project pictures below and the working drawings on page 122. Note how this project primarily requires the use of two special planes: a skew rabbet plane and a small plane for tidying up. We use a Record Skew rabbet No. 712 and a Record bullnose No. 076.

Have a look at the inspirational drawings—on the opposite page—and consider how many exciting variations there are on the sliding-bolt-in-a-groove theme. We also use a lathe—but then again, you could modify this part of the project to match your available tools.

Project pictures—the finished project.

As for the choice of wood, it must be tight grained and easy to plane—like, say, cherry, box, lime, and sycamore.

WOOD LIST

- A 3/4-inch-thick, 3-inch-long slice off the end of a 6-inch-wide plank—so that the grain runs across the width of the catch
- A prepared strip of 3/8-inch-thick wood at 1 5/16 inches wide and 6 inches long, for the sliding bolt
- A scrap of boxwood for the turned knob

TOOLS & MATERIALS

- A skew plane at 1 1/4 inches wide or less
- A small bullnose rabbet plane for tidying up
- A small brass-backed saw—we used a gent's type
- A woodturning lathe fitted with a four-jaw chuck
- A scroll saw
- A holdfast
- A bench drill press
- A 1/2-inch-diameter Forstner drill bit
- A set of woodturning tools that includes:
    a parting tool, a round-nosed scraper, and a small skew chisel
- A pair of calipers
- A quantity of beeswax for burnishing
- A pencil, ruler, and a pair of dividers
- A sheet each of work-out and tracing paper
- All the usual workshop tools and materials . . . sandpaper, PVA glue, holdfast, dividers, scissors, etc.

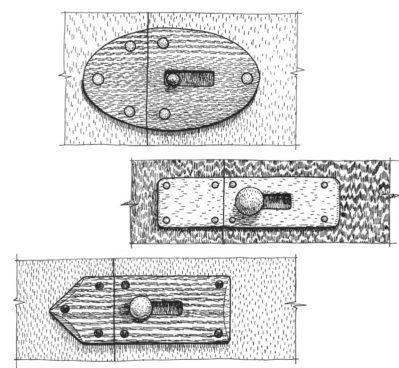

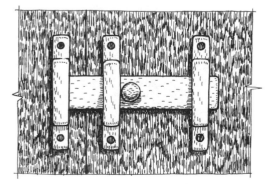

Inspirational designs.
Four alternatives on the captive
bolt theme.

CONSTRUCTION STAGES

Cutting the Groove & Fitting the Sliding Bolt

1. When you have studied the project and collected all your tools and materials, take your chosen wood—the 3 x 6-inch piece with the grain running across the width—establish the best face, and then use the pencil, ruler, and square to set out the position of the groove on the back face.

2. Once you have looked over and checked the working drawings again and you are certain that all of the lines are well placed, take the back saw—or any small saw that you have at hand—and run two cuts down to what will be the base of the groove (*see* 20-1). Run the cuts a little to the waste side of the sides of the groove, and down to the base line.

SPECIAL TIP
Though our old Record skewed rebate plane isn't really designed to cut grooves, it certainly does a beautiful job of it. Our best advice: If you are a beginner on the lookout for tools, buy them secondhand. In our experience old hand tools are less expensive, better quality—and a better all-round deal than new ones.

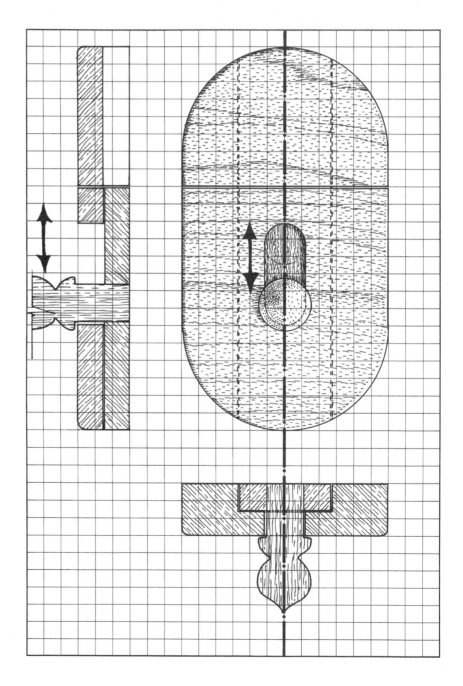

Working drawings—at a grid scale of four squares to an inch.

Note how the success of the project hinges on all the measurements and subsequent cuts being well placed.

20-1 *Only saw down as far as the base line.*

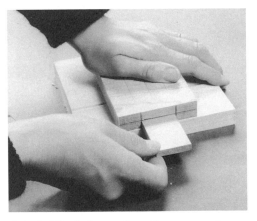

20-2 *Old metallic planes are a joy to use! They are perfect for small projects and they are quick and easy to set up.*

3. Position the workpiece best-face-down on the bench, set a batten alongside the right-hand edge of the groove line—to act as a fence—and then hold the whole works secure with the hold-fast. Once this is in place, then use the skewed rebate plane to sink the groove (*see* 20-2).

4. Having worked the groove, turn and turn about, from both ends—so as not to split off the grain—take the small bullnose plane and clean up. Have a trial fitting with the strip that goes to make the bolt. It needs to be a smooth, easy fit (*see* 20-3). If need be, use the small plane to take a skim off at the edges.

5. The test for a good fit of the sliding bolt is to turn the grooved workpiece over so that the groove becomes a bridge, and then to press down hard on the bridge while at the same time trying to slide the bolt through (*see* 20-4). If it does stick, then take another skim off either the bolt or the groove.

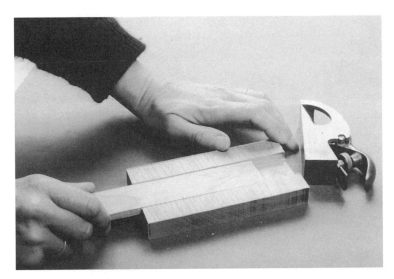

20-3 *Clean off the edges so that the bolt is a smooth, easy fit.*

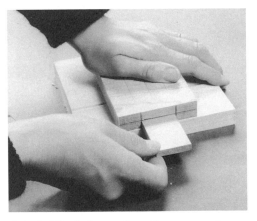

20-4 *The bolt needs to be a smooth, easy fit without being loose and sloppy. Allow for the final sanding and waxing in your calculations.*

20-5 You should finish up with three primary component parts: the two pieces that make the box and the sliding bolt. Now is the time to clean out the corners of the groove.

SHAPING THE BOLT BOX

6. Establish a centerline on the best face of the bolt box, then take the compass and set each end out with a half-circle. If you have stayed with our dimensions, then the half-circle radius will be more or less 1 1/2 inches. While the pencil and ruler are at hand, draw in the line that divides the bolt catch from the main body of the box—it needs to be positioned 2 inches along from the left-hand end of the box. Refer to the top left of the working drawings.

7. When you are sure that all the measurements are just so—it would be a pity to make a mess-up at this late stage!—then move to the scroll saw and cut out the profile. You should finish up with two circle-ended components—one 2 inches long and the other 3 1/2 inches (*see* 20-5).

8. Now it must be said that this stage—meaning locating the position of the little window—is pretty tricky, so take it slowly. Start by fixing the position on the centerline of the two centers—for the two small circles. It's best to locate one center at 3/4 inch along from the left-hand end, and then position the second center 7/8 inch to the right of the first; refer again to the top left of the working drawings.

9. Having scribed out the two circles at a little over 1/2 inch diameter and double-checked, then all you do is run them through with the 1/2 to 9/16-inch Forstner bit and cut the waste away on the scroll saw (*see* 20-6).

10. While at the drill press, set the sliding bolt in place in the groove and run a 1/2-inch-diameter hole straight on through the bolt—that is, at the right-hand end of the window.

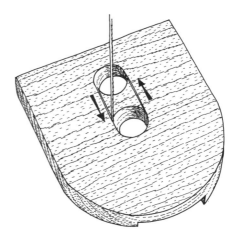

20-6 Check with the working drawings that the two holes are well placed. Be sure to make the saw cuts in the direction of the arrows.

20-7 Be wary at this final stage that you don't crush the tenon in the jaws of the chuck.

TURNING & FINISHING

11. As regards working the little knob, you'd best turn to one or other of the turning projects and take your lead from them. Just remember that apart from the overall form, which can be any shape that takes your fancy, the tenon end of the turning does have to fit your 1/2-inch-diameter hole, and the shoulder of the tenon does have to be something bigger than the box slot. Have a look at the cross-section detail at the top right of the working drawings. Turn the 1/2-inch stalk diameter first—all the rest being cut oversize—and then turn the shoulders down to a good finish at the final stage when the workpiece is in the chuck (*see* 20-7).

12. Finally, rub the works down to a smooth, round-edged finish and burnish it with beeswax.

AFTERTHOUGHTS

- If you can't get to use a lathe, then you can easily modify the design by cutting an Arts & Crafts type knob on the scroll saw. Or you could even whittle a knob.
- The relationship between the knob, the sliding bolt, and the little window is critical. Have a look at the bottom section of the working drawing and note how, when the left-hand end of the sliding bolt is flush with the side of the box, the knob is hard up against the right-hand end of the window and the right-hand end of the bolt is flush with the right-hand end of the box.

• Project 21 •
Chinese Pin Latch

Have a look at the project pictures below and the working drawings and note how this project draws its inspiration directly from a traditional Chinese pin latch. That is to say, there is a central stile with an attached bridge, and two doors—one each side of the stile—each with its own attached bridge. In use, the doors are closed and a long pin is passed through all three bridges, with the effect that the doors are held fast. Don't forget that in a furniture context the bridge strips would need to run through to the top and bottom of the door and the stile.

As regards tools and techniques, you do have to be aware that the greater part of this project has to do with cutting clean, crisp grooves. Note how we use a Stanley 45 multi/combination plane for the grooves. Have a look at the inspirational drawings on the opposite page, and see how there are many designs based on attached bridges and pins.

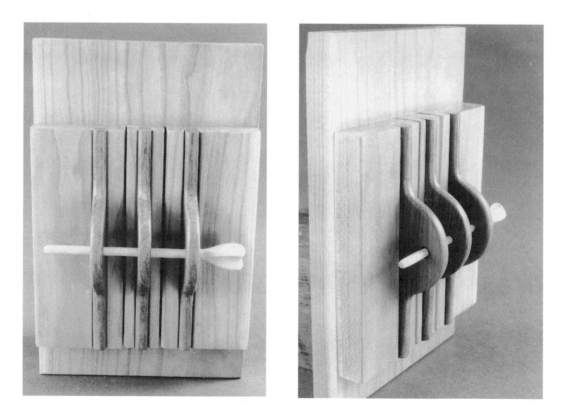

Project pictures—the finished project.

As for the choice of wood—meaning the wood for the bridges, and the pin—not only must they both be tight grained and strong, they also need to be contrasting. We have gone for American cherry for the ground, a dark plum wood for the bridges, and European boxwood for the pin.

WOOD LIST

- A piece of furniture in the making that has a central stile with a door at either side
- A 5/16-inch-thick, 1 1/2-inch-wide strip of plum for each bridge—of a length to suit your piece of furniture
- A 6-inch off-cut of boxwood at about 5/8 x 5/8 inch in cross section

TOOLS & MATERIALS

- A bench fitted with a hold-fast
- A Stanley 45 combination plane (or any other plow-type plane that is able to cut a 5/16-inch-wide groove)
- A small plane for rounding over the edges
- A scroll saw
- A bench drill press
- A 1/4-inch-diameter Forstner drill bit
- A pair of calipers
- A knife for whittling and general tidying up—we use a Swedish sloyd knife
- A quantity of beeswax for burnishing
- A pencil, ruler, and marking gauge
- A sheet each of work-out and tracing paper
- All the usual workshop tools and materials . . . sandpaper, PVA glue, dividers, scissors, etc.

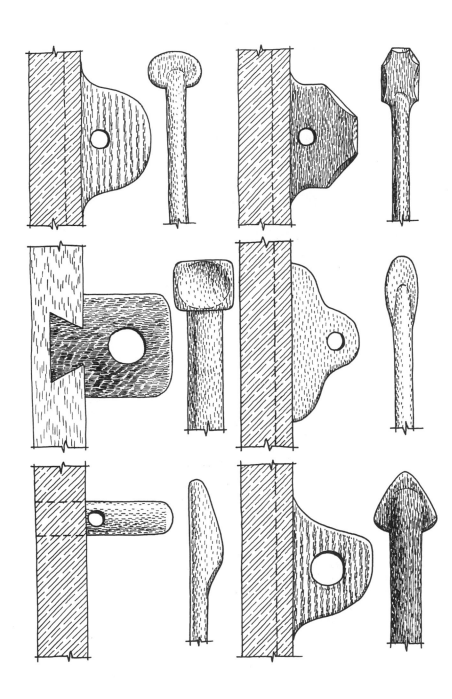

Inspirational designs. Various alternatives on the bridge and rod theme.

CONSTRUCTION STAGES

Setting Out & Cutting the Grooves

1. When you have chosen your wood and had a good long hard look at the working drawings and details, then spend time bringing your plane to good order. In the context of using a Stanley 45, you need to select and hone the 5/16-inch-wide cutting iron and minimize working friction by rubbing the runners and the fence with candle wax.

2. Having brought the plane to good order, take the pencil, ruler, and dividers and set the position of the three grooves out on your piece of furniture. Although of course the precise position of your grooves will almost certainly differ from ours, be sure to stay with the overall spacing and layout. Aim to have the bridges no more than 3/4 inch apart (*see* 21-1).

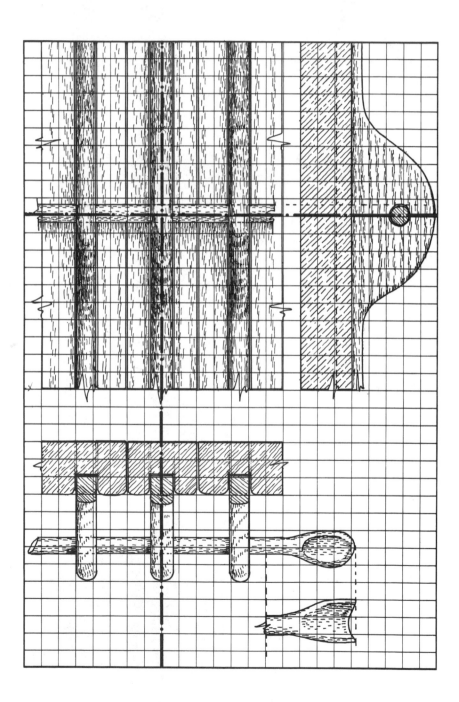

Working drawings—at a grid scale of four squares to an inch.

Note in the cross-section detail how the bridge strips stand proud along their entire length, and the strips and the spaces between the strips are all finished to the same rounded section.

21-1 Although most certainly your piece of furniture will require a different size and arrangement, note how important it is that the spacing be well considered and organized.

21-3 Aim for a constant depth of the grooves.

3. Secure the door or stile flat down on the workbench—so that the groove to be worked is clear of the holdfast, and so that the edge is overhanging the bench. Then set the fence-to-cutter width and the depth gauge foot to suit your design, and begin work. You should aim to lower the grooves to a depth of about 1/4 inch (*see* 21-2).

4. We think that it is a good idea, when you are cutting the grooves, to make repeated soundings with a scrap of "bridge" wood to test for squareness to the surface of the wood, alignment, constant width, and depth. For the best results, the scrap of bridge wood needs to be a tight push-fit and at right angles to the ground (*see* 21-3).

21-2 Note how the workpiece is held secure with the holdfast and with a stop.

21-4 *Drill and fret the stack out, all of a piece, so as to achieve three identical components. Pencil-label each cutout so that you can use it in the same stack sequence.*

CUTTING & FITTING THE BRIDGES

5. Having first had a good long look at the working drawings so that you know where you are heading—take the 5/16-inch-thick 1 1/2-inch-wide strips of wood that you have chosen for the bridges—all cut to length to suit your piece of furniture in the making—and set the design out on one of the three pieces. Make sure that the center point for the pin hole is clearly defined.

6. Shade in the waste so that the cutting line is clearly defined, stack the three pieces together so that the drawn design is uppermost, and then tap a couple of thin pins/nails in the areas of waste—through the whole works.

7. Use the 1/4-inch-diameter Forstner bit to run a hole down through the stack, and then cut the profile out on the scroll saw. If all is well, you should finish up with three identical bridges (*see* 21-4).

8. Have a dry-run fitting with the bridges in the grooves (*see* 21-5). If need be, ease the grooves for a good fit.

21-5 *Ideally the cutouts need to be a tight push-fit.*

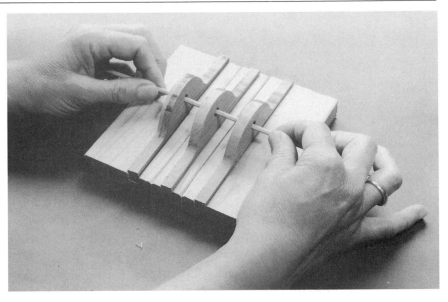

21-6 Assemble the cutouts in the stack sequence so that the holes are perfectly aligned.

ATTACHING & FINISHING

9. Once the whole arrangement comes together for a good fit—so that it is possible to pass a dowel through the three holes (*see* 21-6)—then lightly draw in alignment marks so you know what goes where and how.

10. Use a small plane and/or a knife to round over the edges of the bridges and the edges of the grooves—refer to the bottom cross section of the working drawings.

11. When you come to whittling the pin, then you can go for just about any form that takes your fancy. All that is needed is a dowel-like rod that passes through 1/4-inch holes, with one end coming to a decorative head. (Refer to Project 5 for more guidance.)

12. Finally, rub the entire works down to a smooth finish, glue the bridge pieces in place in the grooves, burnish all the surfaces to a waxed finish, and the job is done.

AFTERTHOUGHTS

- If you can't get to use a Stanley 45 combination plane or indeed any grooving plane, then you could just about get the project made by cutting the grooves with a scoring gauge and a 1/4-inch-wide paring chisel.

- Keeping in mind that the relationship between the three elements is critical—that is, the size and spacing of the bridges, and the diameter of the pin—if you do decide to go for something larger or smaller, you will have to size everything to fit. So, for example, if you want to go for twice the size, then everything needs to be scaled up accordingly.

- If you find that you enjoy cutting grooves and rebates, and tongues, and reeds, and all the other profiles that go to make woodwork so exciting, then you could do yourself a favor and buy a secondhand Stanley 45 Combination plane.

• Project 22 •

Sliding Dovetail Latch

Have a look at the project pictures below and the working drawings, and consider how this project needs to be made on a scroll saw. Or to be even more specific, this project needs to be made on a scroll saw that has an angle table function. I say this because if you look at the working drawings, you will see that the shape and design of the sliding dovetail latch is such that it can only really be cut when the worktable is canted over at an angle to the blade.

Have a look at the inspirational drawings—on the opposite page—and see how there are many possible designs that make use of the sliding dovetail theme.

As regards the choice of wood, this project will only really work if you use a tight-grained strong wood—one that has strength when it is cut down to a relatively slender thickness of about 5/16 inch. We have gone for English plum.

Project pictures—the finished project.

WOOD LIST
- A sophisticated piece of furniture that needs a feature latch
- A 5/16-inch-thick piece of plum at about 5 1/2 x 5 1/2 inches

TOOLS & MATERIALS
- A scroll saw with an angle table capability
- A bench drill press
- Forstner drill bits at 1/4-inch and 3/4-inch diameter
- A pair of calipers
- A compass
- A knife for whittling and general tidying up—we use a Swedish sloyd knife
- A quantity of beeswax for burnishing
- A pencil and ruler
- A sheet each of work-out and tracing paper
- All the usual workshop tools and materials . . . sandpaper, PVA glue, dividers, scissors, etc.

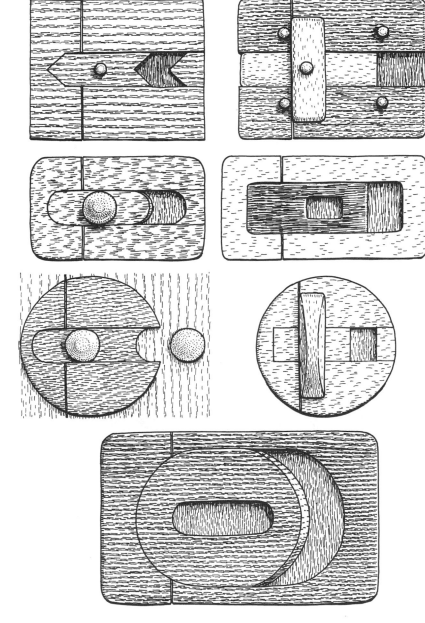

Inspirational designs. Various alternatives on the sliding dovetail idea.

CONSTRUCTION STAGES

Setting Out the Circle & Cutting the Blank

1. When you are sure that your scroll saw is up to the task, have a close-up look at your chosen piece of wood and see that it is tight grained and strong, and generally free from knots, warping, and splits. If it is faulted in any way, then now is the time to search out another piece.

2. Having first selected the best face, set your compass or dividers to a radius of 2 1/2 inches and strike off a 5-inch-diameter circle (*see* 22-1). It's important that you get it right the first time around—no scratches or deep marks.

3. In the context that plum is an amazingly dense, difficult-to-cut wood, then now is the time to fit the scroll saw with a new fine-toothed blade and to adjust the blade tension so that it is somewhat over-strung. Once this is done, then very carefully fret out the shape so that the line of cut is slightly to the waste side of the drawn line (*see* 22-2).

Working drawings—at a grid scale of four squares to an inch.

Have a look at the two cross-section details and note how the angled edge of the latch cants out from the best face so that the angled overhang of the plate holds and contains the latch.

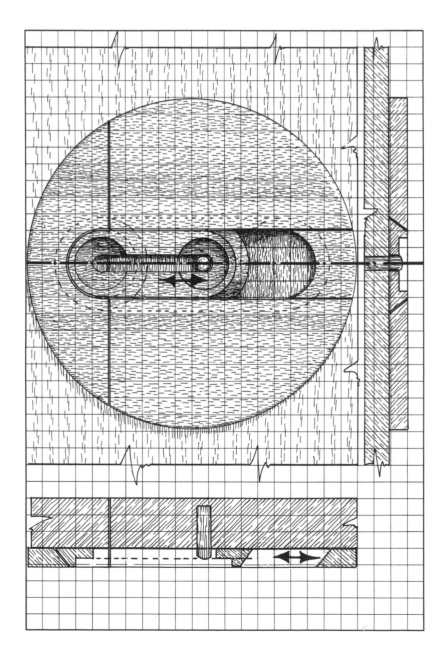

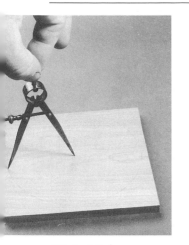

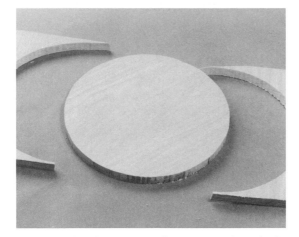

22-1 *Make sure that the divider arm is well spiked on the center point.*

22-2 *If by chance your line of cut does deviate from the drawn line, then at least make sure that the misplaced cut is on the waste side of the drawn line.*

22-3 *Note that we decided to alter the design, as indicated by the shading—modifying as we worked.*

SETTING OUT & CUTTING THE DOVETAIL LATCH

4. Having drawn out the design (*see* 22-3), we decided not to cut out the shaded area, but rather to have the half-circle curve the other way. Use the pencil, ruler, and compass to draw in the centerline, the line that defines the side of the door, and the 1-inch-wide circle-ended shape that marks out the latch. Note that the grain must run from side to side across the circle—along the length of the latch.

5. When you are sure that all the guidelines are well placed, adjust the scroll saw table to an angle of about 45 degrees and set to work fretting out the shape (*see* 22-4). Make certain that you have the angle of the dovetail canted back from the best face.

6. If all is well, the latch should be held captive by the overhang of the surrounding plate (*see* 22-5).

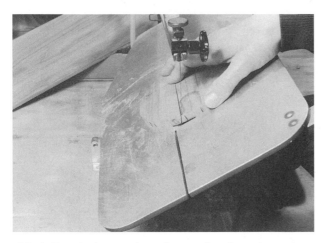

22-4 *Don't forget that the angle of cut must be canted down and out from the best face.*

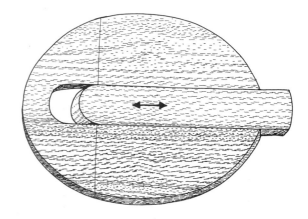

22-5 *See how the latch is held in place by the overhanging surround.*

MODELING & DETAILING THE LATCH

7. Draw in the position of the cutting line that defines the other end of the latch, and mark out the area of waste that needs cutting back. If you have drawn it correctly, the two small circle center points should be about 2 inches apart—refer to the working drawings.

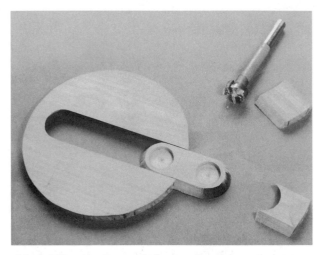

22-6 *The two finger holes need to be sunk to a level of about 1/8 inch.*

8. With all the guidelines in place, use the 3/4-inch-diameter Forstner bit to sink two holes about halfway through the thickness of the wood, and use the scroll saw to fret the other end of the latch and trim away the piece of waste (*see* 22-6).

9. Run a 1/4-inch-diameter hole through each of the centers, then flip the catch over, draw two parallel lines to link the 1/4-inch holes, and afterwards clear the waste on the scroll saw (*see* 22-7). Though this is a pretty straightforward procedure, you do have to remember that, as the line of cut runs through two different thicknesses of wood, the rate of cut will suddenly change.

FITTING & FINISHING

10. When you have decided whereabouts on your door and stile you want the project to be located, set the component parts in place—with the latch closed—and use a pencil to transfer the center point at the right-hand end of the latch through to the base board. This done, run a 1/4-inch-diameter hole about 1/2 inch down into the base board. Push a short length of dowel in the hole for a trial fitting (*see* 22-8).

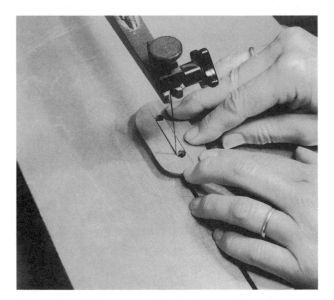

22-7 *In this instance the design and cutting are best managed from the back face of the workpiece.*

22-8 *Set the small dowel stub so that it is at a slightly lower level than the bottom of the finger holes.*

22-9 Prior to gluing, set the component parts down and see how they can be brought together and adjusted so that the latch is a tight fit. It's always a good idea to play around with the arrangement before you ever put glue to wood.

11.　Finally, bring the five components together (*see* 22-9), and when you are happy that the latch is a good smooth-running fit, use the finest sandpaper to rub down the sawn faces and edges; then glue the whole works in place on your furniture and burnish it with beeswax.

AFTERTHOUGHTS

- If you can't get to use a scroll saw, then you could use a fine-bladed hand piercing saw or even a hand fret saw. Either way, the blade needs to be fine.
- Don't forget that the wood must be tight grained and resistant to splits. Something like boxwood, maple, cherry, or pear would be just fine.
- You do have to be careful, when you are fretting the latch out at an angle, that you don't finish up with the angle running in the wrong direction. Give it a lot of thought before you start sawing.
- As the dovetail catch is small and flush-fitting, so is it particularly suited for situations where you want the minimum of bits sticking out—for example, with small cupboards and for small compartments in desks.

• Project 23 •
Leaf Spring Latch

Have a look at the project pictures below and the working drawings, and note how this project is made almost entirely on a small band saw. Consider also how the design is excitingly unusual, in that the sliding latch is held and returned by two thin strips of wood—called a leaf spring. In use, the latch is slid to the right to open, and then of course when you let go of the knob, the leaf spring shoots the latch back in place.

Have a look at the inspirational drawings on the opposite page. Note how many possible designs there are that use the leaf spring idea.

Regarding the choice of wood, the leaf spring needs to be made of a wood type that is springy and strong along the length of the grain. We used American oak for the main body and for the latch, and a strip each of ash and poplar for the leaf spring. We chose two wood types, just in case one type let us down.

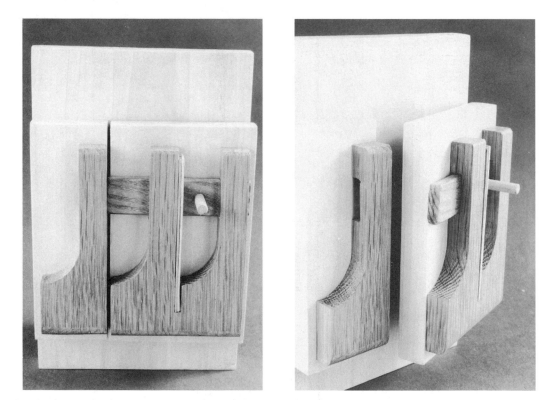

Project pictures—the finished project.

WOOD LIST

- A piece of furniture or maybe a large door in the making that needs a latch
- A 3/4-inch-thick piece of oak at about 6 x 6 inches—for the body of the latch
- A 3/8-inch-thick strip of oak or ash at 1 inch wide and 6 inches long—for the latch
- A couple of 1/16-inch-thick strips of springy wood at about 3/4 inch wide and 5 inches long—for the leaf springs

TOOLS & MATERIALS

- A small band saw with a 1/4-inch-wide fine-toothed blade—small enough to cut the curves
- A small shoulder or nosing-type plane for cleaning out the groove
- A bevel-edged paring chisel at 3/4 to 1 inch wide
- A bench drill press
- A 1/4-inch-diameter Forstner drill bit
  - A fine-toothed back saw—we use a gent's
- A pair of calipers
- A knife for whittling and general tidying up—we use a Swedish sloyd knife
- A quantity of beeswax for burnishing
- A pencil and ruler
- A sheet each of work-out and tracing paper
- All the usual workshop tools and materials . . . sandpaper, PVA glue, dividers, scissors, etc.

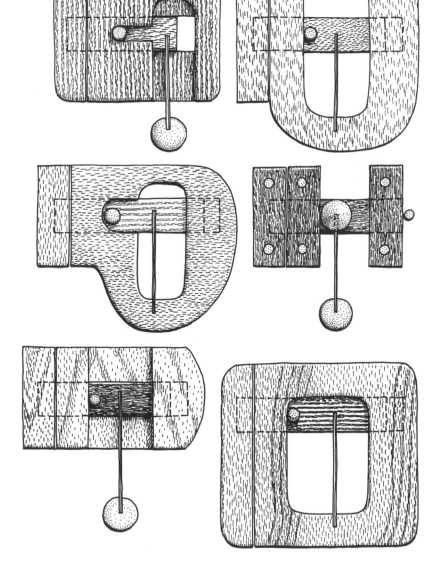

Inspirational designs. Various alternatives that use leaf springs in their design.

CONSTRUCTION STAGES

Setting Out the Design & Cutting the Groove

1. When you have a clear understanding of how the project needs to be worked, take your 6 x 6-inch piece of 3/4-inch-thick oak and cut it down to a finished size of 5 1/4 inches wide and 5 inches high. Have the grain up and down—along the length.

2. Having pencil-marked the best face and the top edge, study our working drawings, and then use the pencil, ruler, and compass to set the design out on the wood. Draw the fancy profile out on the best face and the groove out on the back.

3. Now, flip the wood over so that the back side is uppermost, and then use the fine saw to set each side of the groove in with a 3/8-inch-deep kerf—that is, a saw cut. Have the cuts to the waste side of the drawn lines, so that the total width of the groove is 1 inch.

4. Butt the workpiece hard up against a bench hook or stop—so that the groove is looking away from you—and use the chisel to pare out the waste. First angle the sides of the waste down into the bottom of the saw cut and then skim off the resultant peak (*see* 23-1). Skim in from the ends towards the middle—so as not to damage the grain at the ends of the groove.

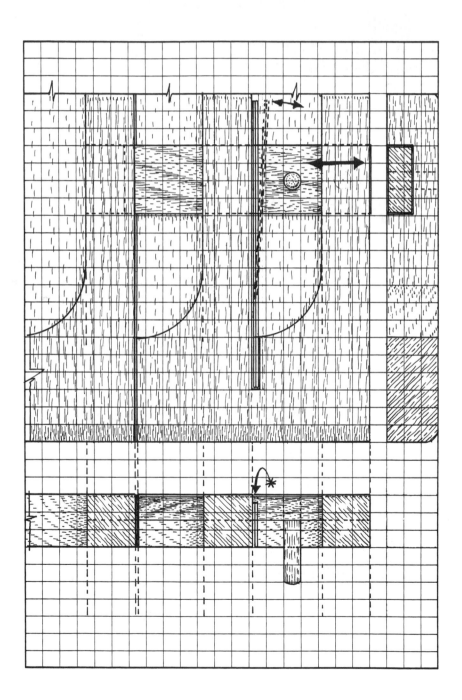

Working drawings—at a grid scale of four squares to an inch.
Have a look at the details and note how the success of the latch has to do with the leaf springs. Don't let the edges of the springs drag on the door at the point marked with an asterisk.

140

23-1 *A 3/4-inch chisel leaves room to maneuver in the 1-inch-wide groove.*

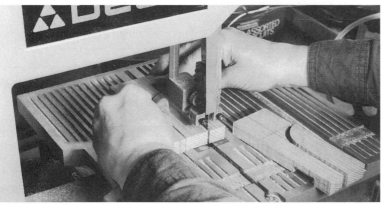

23-3 *Never have your fingers close to the front of the band saw blade. It's best to push within, say, 3 to 5 inches, and then either drag the workpiece through or use push sticks.*

5. When you have pared down to within a whisker of the required depth, then use the plane to clean up. Continue until the latch strip is a smooth-running fit in the groove, and until the upper face of the strip is set at a slightly lower level than the upper face of the surrounding wood (*see 23-2*).

CUTTING THE LATCH BOX & FITTING THE LEAF SPRINGS

6. Move to the band saw and set to work cutting out the profile of the latch box. Keeping in mind that the curves need to be cut with care and precision, start by having a tryout on some scrap wood—to see if your blade is small enough to go around the curve.

7. When all is well, then carefully cut out the profile as shown in the working drawings and 23-3. You should finish up with two component parts.

23-2 *(Left) Clean out the corners of the groove and plane off the corners of the latch strip—until the movement runs smoothly.*

SPECIAL TIP
We're always cautious when working on the band saw, simply because it is so unforgiving. If something goes wrong, then the mess-up is likely to be swift and messy! For this project, you have to watch out when you are cutting across the groove, because at the moment when the blade goes from cutting thick wood to cutting thin, there is a sudden increase in the speed of cut. It could be dangerous—so be on your guard!

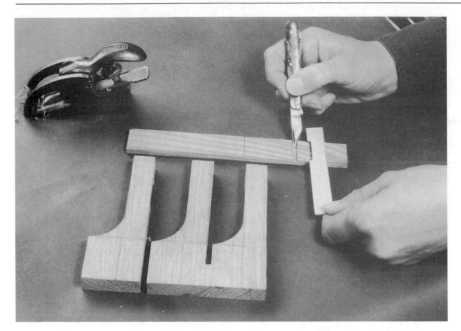

23-4 *Cut and notch both components so that they interlock—and so that the bottom edge of the spring strip doesn't drag on the door.*

8. Having sawn out the two parts, slide the latch strip and the two spring strips in place, and mark the intersection. Make a couple of side-by-side saw cuts across the latch and take a notch out of the spring strip—so that they interlock (*see* 23-4).

9. Play around with the precise location of the leaf spring—that is, try various thicknesses and widths of wood—until you are pleased with the way the latch works (*see* 23-5).

SPECIAL TIP
If the spring catches or fails to push the latch back, then chances are it is pressed down too hard along its length, with the effect that its edge is dragging on the front of the door. The whole working action will smooth out once the various faces have been burnished with beeswax.

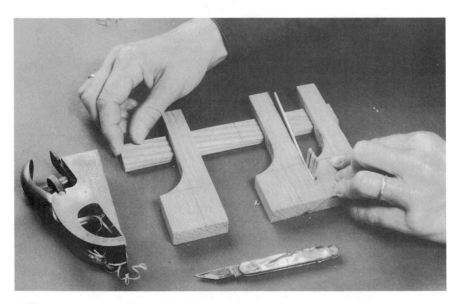

23-5 *You will have to try out various combinations of fit and wood type for the leaf springs before you get it right.*

PUTTING TOGETHER & FINISHING

10. When you are happy with the action of the latch and spring, smear a small amount of glue in the slot and attach the leaf springs in place with a glued sliver of wood.

11. Cut the latch strip to length and drill and fit the dowel knob. Remember that the knob needs to be placed so that it also acts as a stop— to keep you over-stretching and breaking the leaf spring.

12. Round over all the edges, use the fine-grade sandpaper to rub down to a smooth finish, ease the groove to allow for the slight curved movement of the latch strip, burnish with beeswax, and the latch is ready for fitting.

AFTERTHOUGHTS

• If you can't get to use a band saw, then you could simply use a scroll saw or even a hand coping saw.

• Don't forget that the wood used for the springs must be strong and springy along the run of the grain. We obtained our wood from a sawmill wood supplier—the 1/16-inch-thick strips were off-cuts left over after another customer's wood was trimmed to size. Although we tried all manner of wood types, thicknesses, and laminations, we settled in the end for two strips—one of ash and one of poplar—placed side by side, and only glued and wedged at the bottom end.

Index